Praise for *Undisciplined*

'Coming from an undisciplined scholar who has been in the movement, *Undisciplined* offers a wide-ranging contribution that implores us to think and read differently.'

Remi Joseph-Salisbury, author of
Anti-Racist Scholar-Activism

'*Undisciplined* is both an intimate invitation and a vivid journey towards and with freedom. Melz Owusu offers rousing reflections on movement work and the alchemy of imagination, love, and action that makes meaningful forms of change and knowing possible. This vital book includes crucial insights and offerings related to the heart and soul, learning and remembering, philosophy and spirituality, and the material and immaterial makings of another world. *Undisciplined* may move and support you in ways you did not know you needed. This book is a freeing force that I will turn to time and time again.'

Francesca Sobande, co-editor of *To Exist is to Resist*

'The central question of *Undisciplined* is: how did this world come to be made and how do we unmake it? A meditative, lyrical work, at once personal and expansive, *Undisciplined* is as relevant to the individual as it is to the (anti-)institutional. Owusu encourages us to be and think outside of the strictures of our current possibilities in favour of a belief in, and commitment to, making the intentions and dreams of the marginalized tangible.'

Rianna Walcott, Founder of Project Myopia

T0243785

Undisciplined

Undisciplined

Reclaiming the Right to Imagine

MELZ OWUSU

polity

First published in 2025 by Polity Press

Polity Press
65 Bridge Street
Cambridge CB2 1UR, UK

Polity Press
111 River Street
Hoboken, NJ 07030, USA

ISBN-13: 978-1-5095-5635-9
ISBN-13: 978-1-5095-5636-6(pb)

A catalogue record for this book is available from the British Library.

Library of Congress Control Number: 2024936121

Typeset in 11 on 14pt Warnock Pro
by Cheshire Typesetting Ltd, Cuddington, Cheshire
Printed and bound in Great Britain by CPI Group (UK) Ltd, Croydon

The publisher has used its best endeavours to ensure that the URLs for external websites referred to in this book are correct and active at the time of going to press. However, the publisher has no responsibility for the websites and can make no guarantee that a site will remain live or that the content is or will remain appropriate.

Every effort has been made to trace all copyright holders, but if any have been overlooked the publisher will be pleased to include any necessary credits in any subsequent reprint or edition.

For further information on Polity, visit our website:
politybooks.com

Contents

Acknowledgements

Firstly, I would like to acknowledge and thank myself. I don't think people do that enough, so thank you Melz. Thank you for holding the discipline to make this work possible alongside your doctoral studies at Cambridge and running the Free Black University. Thank you for always standing firm in what you believe in, no matter the backlash. Thank you for spending the past decade of your life committed to the decolonial question, for demanding more for yourself in the space of learning and more for others. I am deeply proud of you. Thank you for following the deepest calling of your heart and soul, and allowing yourself to expand into your purpose for the stage of life that this work reflects.

Thank you to my family and friends. My anchors through this world. Thank you to my mum, my Auntie Andrea and by big sister Natasha. You all helped raise me, and allow me to know that whatever happens in this world, I am deeply loved. It is only from this foundation that I feel able to think, to write, to create. Thank you to my friend of almost 20 years Eniola Fetuga – you mean the world to me, thank you for being the safest space to land. Thank you to Taiwo Ogunyinka, my right-hand man forever and always, thank you for believing in my visions and helping me bring them to fruition. Over the years your support has meant the world, from the simplest of things like cooking for me at my lowest points, to running the Free Black University alongside me. Thank you to my dear friend Nathan Bryant – you opened a whole world to me when you suggested we watch that film about ancestral practices across Africa all those years ago, that took me on a journey that led me here. Thank you, Uncle Perry, for always believing in me and encouraging me in the exact way I need; your words consistently keep the fire within me burning.

Thank you to every person that chose the continued discipline of writing worlds into being. Thank you to those writers, thinkers and world benders that showed me more is possible. Thank you to Audre Lorde, to bell hooks, to Steve Biko, to Patricia Hill Collins, to Frantz Fanon, to Huey P. Newton, to Akwake Emezi, to Sabonfu Somé, to Malidoma Patrice Somé, to Octavia Butler, to adrienne maree brown and so so many more.

Thank you to the Free Black University, an organisation I founded with support from my community in 2020; thank you to everyone that was a part of its birthing, its team and especially our students. Each and every student taught me of a new possibility, a possibility that helped me both write and believe in the worlds held in these pages.

Thank you to everyone that has supported my work, everyone that has inspired me to believe that we can transform the world. Thank you to Nathaniel Tobias ~~Coleman~~, to Kayza Rose, to Farzana Khan, to Temi Mwale, to Liv Little, to Ama Josephine Budge, and to so many more. Thank you to my spiritual guides, to my mentors and teachers, and to those I watch from afar and remain inspired by.

Finally, thank you to the woman that taught me many things about love as I penned the final pages of this book.

Thank you.

For Palestine

*

For Shay
Our Trans Sibling Watching Over Us

*

For Melissa
I Am You; You Are Me.
Thank You.

Introduction

The only way to deal with an unfree world is to become so absolutely free that your very existence is an act of rebellion.

— Albert Camus

What struck me the most, was how much I grew as a person through the process of writing this book. I believe the purpose of life is to do what you love, and to be transformed by the journey. This book is a gentle offering of that way of living.

Undisciplined is a book about knowledge. It is a journey through epistemology, the philosophical study of knowledge itself, the study of how knowledge is created, validated, and justified. We open with an exploration of the production of knowledge in the modern world through an analysis of the University as a focal point through which 'valid' knowledge is created and disseminated. With this, I journey through my own experiences within the academy, and explore the ways in which the academy has the capacity to pull one away from their ability to imagine, and the ability to be the verifier of their own truth(s). I consider how we might go about rediscovering, through a decolonial lens, our most radical imaginations and how entangled this rediscovery of one's imagination is with the ability to engage with epistemology *differently*.

The intention of this work is not necessarily to convince you. Indeed, it is a worthy by-product of my mission if you are convinced by the arguments made throughout. However, the core intention is instead to encourage you to feel, to deeply feel, and be transformed by whatever this work stirs within you.

If I wake up one day in a challenging mood or in a vibrant mood, some way or another it will find its way to permeate my work. It is dishonest to make the claim that there is any separation between me and my work, and thus I lean into that throughout *Undisciplined*, as opposed to away from it. Equally, whether your heart is open or whether it is closed upon arriving at the reading of this book will influence the experience you have of it. There is no right or wrong here, just a complex web of feeling, being, and existing – stay with whatever arises.

Undisciplined is a journey from narrating and critiquing the nature of the education system and knowledge system that underwrites it, to embracing and recognising the profound liberatory potential of spirituality, imagination, and love.

We begin with the exploration of the University as a site of discipline and explore how coloniality and the education system teaches and shames one out of their own imagination. Fundamentally, the argument for the abolition of the University is made. As the book shifts, bends, and expands, we move our focus from the University and into the potential a decolonial approach, which regards spirituality as a site of knowledge production, has in remedying some of the concerns outlined in the earlier chapters. Following this, I explore my own queerness and transness as a site of knowledge production and a central way to consider the value of one's interior life, a life that exists in the realm of the unseen, as a valid and valuable site of knowledge production. We close with love as a refrain to navigate the space between the world of form, and the world of the immaterial, and consider abolition as an act of remembering through the lens of our souls. This is to suggest that the reason we *fight for* and *know* a more just world is possible is because that knowing is inscribed within our souls.

Undisciplined is a journey from undisciplining the mind and body, to recognising the existence of, and building connection with, the spirit and soul. *Undisciplined* asks us what a truly holistic and embodied approach to healing ourselves and the world through the gateway of the heart may look, feel, and taste like.

This book weaves through deep intellectual arguments, to personal and spiritual reflections. It is not a requirement to read it as a manual: go where your heart calls you to.

The book is not instructive in the traditional sense; I offer my reflections as one possible discourse or approach to the work that I am concerned with. I offer it with the encouragement and welcoming of challenge to my thesis and positioning – if it is not in alignment with your own life and truth, release it.

There is no one single way we all get free, just a complex web of *beautiful experiments*, as Saidiya Hartman might put it.

Receive this as an offering of my own experiment – the findings are not as important as the process, as the journey.

This book is an attempt to bring together the lessons I have learnt over a decade of considering the question of 'decoloniality' as both a movement worker and as an intellectual. It is an attempt to honour the journey that it has taken me on in its truest expression, and how my spiritual life is core to the decolonial question.

This is a book about knowledge, it is about our ancestors. This is a book about freedom, it is about how we might reconsider our relationship to justice.

This book considers the immaterial journey towards liberation as just as important as work in the material world. This is a book that asks not only how we move into more just futures, but who we must become to live in and sustain the worlds we long for.

This book is a love letter.

Author's Note

I have chosen to use the first names, as opposed to surnames, of all the thinkers I work with throughout this book; this has been done with the intention of breaking down hierarchies. I remember during high school I asked my history teacher why we refer to people in history using their surnames; I found it absurd. He responded by telling me he actually doesn't know. I've come to feel that it is a practice that creates and reproduces hierarchies of power inside and outside of the academy. If I converse with someone that I perceive as being at the same level as me, I use their first name; it is only when I converse with someone that may be of a higher professional post or age, or someone that is simply distant from me, I use their surname with a prefix. Yes, this is often to signify respect, but for me respect is something that is earnt at a personal level not something that can be conferred by a scholarly community, or society at large.

So, I believe this practice operates to demonstrate and reinforce the hierarchies at play within institutions and society. To place oneself below, and the other above. I feel this practice is also reflective of a patriarchal norm that often goes undetected, as surnames are, for the most part, inherited through the paternal line, or taken on at marriage by the woman in heterosexual relationships. Thus, this further cements a sense of male dominance in the academy and how we re-present and therefore consider history. I have taught too many students who have said to me that they feel they have nothing of worth to say, and question why their voices should or could stand up against the thinkers they write about. I have to remind them that these figures, these thinkers, are human just like them, and I contend that a way to consistently remember this is by using the first name. I am in equitable conversation with these thinkers and historical figures, and so all in-text mentions of thinkers and historical figures are on a first-name basis.

Ultimately, for me, to utilise first names is to be in a conversation that is insubordinate, non-hierarchical, balanced, and, fundamentally, a conversation that is *Undisciplined*.

1

The Undisciplined

The Possibility of Another World

My first degree was in Philosophy and Politics. There was a Philosophy class that I took during my second year of study that I often come back to; it was a part of a module in Advanced Logic. The class posed the question of other possible worlds. These other worlds were conceptually offered by the lecturer as *other canonical models*. That there is a possibility that various and infinite worlds exist beyond our perception and ability to quantify. Further, that the canons or laws that govern these worlds both in the natural world and by way of philosophical principles, may be entirely different. I was fascinated. It brought a new possibility into my personal world, the idea that everything could be entirely different. It was probably not the aim of the lecture, but it played a significant part in reshaping my relationship to activism and the change I longed to see in the world. Rather than believing change is limited to this canonical model, what may happen if we move to anchor other possible canonical models, specifically focused on foundational philosophical principles that govern our minds, bodies, and how we relate to one another, into this physical world? If those worlds have the possibility of existing, then there is equally a possibility that this world could be reshaped and reformed from its very core. That it no longer must just be about reforming this system, it became about creating entirely new worlds and visions of freedom that are not anchored to what is considered 'possible' within our current canonical model. The 'impossible' became possible.

We are collectively shifting into new dimensions and understandings of collective liberation and freedom. The old paradigm of reforming the system through the pleas for small justices within archaic and oppressive systems are falling away. Instead, abolition has become a part of the collective consciousness. This was no clearer than during the uprisings of 2020 that erupted across North America, the United Kingdom, and in pockets across Europe and the rest of the world. After the murder of George Floyd in Minneapolis, there was an outpouring of abolitionist education through social media. I was a witness to, and was a part of, the discussions during the summer and autumn months of 2020 as abolitionist rhetoric became a part of the collective conversation, and the freedom dreaming that was being explored on a mass scale was ever expanding. The abolitionist step to call for the defunding of the police, a phrase popularised by the Black Visions Collective, who are a radical Black LGBTQ+-led organising group based in Minnesota (Wortham, 2020), was discussed on mainstream news channels across the world (Levin, 2020; Zaru and Simpson, 2020; BBC News, 2020b).

It felt as though we were standing at the gateway of another world. A possibility that existed beyond what we are educated to believe is achievable, it felt we might be able to shape and create new worlds. For me, abolition is the demand for a new world. It is not simply the call to end the prison and policing systems, or any other harmful institutions. It is a call to entirely reshape and recreate the world from its foundations. Nothing can be abolished in isolation; the implications of the end of any system require us to rethink and reshape the world as we know it.

Abolition is about beginnings, not just endings.

What beauty and possibility may erupt in the wake of the endings? What may be birthed through the fertile ground the abolitionist movement lays down? In the seminal text *Are Prisons Obsolete?* Angela Davis (2003) offered us an evaluation of the abolition of the prison, firstly by contextualising it in the rich history of abolition for African Americans from slavery to Civil Rights. She demonstrates that what at the time many would have considered impossible to change, such as the institutions of slavery and Jim Crow, are now no longer enshrined in US law, and so in a similar way we might collectively imagine a world beyond the prison. In this she argued that we must reimagine society as a whole and begin working towards that societal transformation to reach the place of rendering the prison obsolete.

Since then, we have had an emerging school of critical literature which places attention on the prison as a site for which abolitionist dreams can and must be realised (Gilmore, 2007; Kaba, 2021). Here, I take the prison as the critical location that it is, but importantly also as a metaphor, as a fungible tool through which we may deepen our understanding of all within the world outside of the physical location of the prison that incarcerates and controls. As such, through the lens of the prison we can understand the ways that we are disciplined and controlled within 'free' society. This is explored in Steven Dillon's (2016) contribution to the edited volume *Captive Genders: Trans Embodiment and the Prison Industrial Complex* wherein he explored the concept of freedom and unfreedoms with trans prisoners through the art of letter writing. The prisoners who he refers to as C and R recognise 'the free world as intimately connected to and constituted by the prison, and further that free world is anything but free; rather, it is an extension of . . . unfreedom' (p. 196). He goes on to explore that the prisoners see death as freedom as opposed to release back into the 'free' world. Steven argues this is the epistemology (knowledge system) required to fight against formations of power that exceed the boundaries of liberalism. By this, Steven is suggesting that we not only must fight against the Prison Industrial Complex and render the institutions of prisons and policing obsolete – but we must also challenge the liberal epistemology that suggests any of us living outside of the prison's gates are free at all. What Steven's work here, as well as in his *Fugitive Life: The Queer Politics of the Prison State* (2018), offers is the understanding that prisons shape our relationship to our own subjectivities as 'free'. The separation and juxtaposition the prison offers as a comparative site of unfreedom in 'civil society' services the implication that those outside of the prison's gates are 'free'. Yet, as stated, this freedom is a fallacy, and therefore the prison produces a dichotomy that essentially legitimises the unfreedoms we experience outside of the prison's gates. In turn, this limits our ability to imagine freedoms beyond the confines of the modern world because the epistemology of the Liberal State tells us we are already free. In a similar vein Joy James (2013) offers, in her conception of Afrarealism, a mode of thinking that critiques Black philosophy from a Black feminist and womanist standpoint on its ability to conceptualise freedom that, 'in fantasies of democracy, the enslaver rescues the savage from barbarity, and the abolitionist saves the savage from the enslaver. Afrarealism sees both forms of "salvation" as captivity' (p. 125). These offerings demonstrate that freedom is not just a question of material reality; it is also a question of consciousness.

Freedom and Consciousness

We cannot mobilise towards freedom if we are not conscious of how unfree we truly are. Historically the concept of freedom is a contested category – philosophers, politicians, historians, activists, sociologists, and indeed the general population have debated and complexly considered what it truly means to be free. The question of *freedom* is a conversation that every person has a stake in. Western philosophers of the liberal tradition have offered some of the most influential (read: dominating) conceptualisations of freedom with regard to how we construct society. John Stuart Mill (2016) offers the concept of liberty as freedom from constraints on the basis that this freedom from constraint does not infringe on another's liberty. Isiah Berlin (1969) develops this and argues John's conception of freedom is negative freedom and there is also positive freedom, which pertains to a person's ability to act freely and take control of their own life. Both approaches to freedom are deeply entrenched in the individual as a product of Western individualist thought. As mentioned, Steven Dillon (2016) offers that C and R, from their positionality within the constraints of the prison cell, do not consider release back into the 'free' (read: unfree) world as freedom, even though within a country governed by Western Liberal Democracy they should conceivably have greater access to both positive and negative freedom to live out their lives as they so wish. Though instead the only freedom C and R can conceptualise is in the afterlife. We are often taught to hold freedom comparatively – what I mean by this is that the comparison of the prison vs. the free world teaches that by comparison we are free. Also, that freedom is something that the individual can largely gain alone and maintain alone by virtue of personal responsibility.

The zeitgeist of modern freedom is arguably to be financially free; the internet is inundated with videos, articles, and think-pieces on the topic. Still, the age-old adage of the wealthy remains that 'money does not bring about happiness'. So, can we be truly free if we are not happy and fulfilled? Connection, community, love, safety, belonging, are arguably some of the key tenets of living a fulfilled life, though all these experiences require others and cannot be fulfilled as an individual alone. As such, freedom should not be held comparatively – e.g., prison vs. the free world, poverty vs. riches – instead, I argue it should be held complexly. We should hold freedom with an open heart – by this I mean that to believe we can offer something as expansive and spacious as freedom a definitive definition is to misunderstand the concept of freedom altogether. This incongruity is a demonstration of a knowledge system that cannot cope with uncertainty and has an insatiable colonising desire to *know*. To aim to define freedom is to counter-intuitively place it within linguistic chains, to pull and package something that should, by its very essence, be free. The effervescence of freedom should be embraced not controlled or captured. With this, holding freedom with an openness that extends from the heart allows us to understand it is an ever-expanding concept which offers us the right to recognise that we are allowed to imagine freedom beyond whatever parameters are offered to us. Hence, we may become as free as our consciousness of both our current freedoms and unfreedoms allows us to be. For if we can imagine and conceptualise a sense of freedom beyond our current conditions, we are developing in consciousness through the eye of our imagination. Still, we must recognise that whenever we may step into the freedoms imagined from this space, the act of liberation offers us a new vantage point from which we may be able to imagine a deeper sense of freedom and begin the journey towards that. The potential and possibilities of freedom are unending – our relationship to freedom continues to develop as our consciousness of our conditions and what may lay beyond that also develops. If our perception holds that all that is possible beyond the prison gates is the world as we know it, one would hold that we have reached freedoms' ends in Western Liberal Democracy. What does it mean to demand more of freedom? To become conscious of the unfreedoms that surround us and be brave and daring enough to imagine more for the world, for ourselves, and for our communities. This is the work of consciousness raising.

Historically, Black Consciousness movements have been heralded at the helm of Black liberation fronts. I have personally been transformed through learning about the Black Consciousness movements in the United States of America through the 1960s and 1970s, the Black Consciousness movements across Africa that led to the end of land colonisation, and perhaps most pertinently the Black Consciousness movement in South Africa that led to the end of apartheid. Student activist and radical thinker Steve Biko (1987) is cited as the founder of the South African Black Consciousness movement. Through the reading of *I Write What I Like*, a collection of Steve's essays, I came to understand what consciousness meant, and the importance of a consciousness movement to give a home and offer a foundation to any radical work that is to be done. Steve's work brought to life so many lines of inquiry that I had not consciously fully embraced into my life and my work. The way he was able to use such clear and direct language to assess the power relations of apartheid, and especially the role that liberalism played in this, was profound. I do not mention this to explore his specific arguments, but more so to offer an understanding to the role and power of consciousness raising. It is the offering of language and analysis to the workings of structural and epistemological power. It illuminates what before may have been mired in the smoke of colonial confusion and the rhetoric which tells us we are free, but the quiet realities of unfreedom that we experience but may not be able to 'put our finger on' or clearly articulate. This is how systems of unfreedom continue to hold their hegemony: we organise strategic and intentional fights against what we are not able to articulate. Hence, consciousness movements have been indispensable to the expansion and development of radical movements. It is through consciousness that we gain direction and then are able to travel to different planes of understanding and open up alternative canons of knowledge through which the birthing of new worlds becomes possible.

When I sit to read a book like *I Write What I Like*, written by someone who has passed on to the afterlife, I see it both as an intellectual act but also as a spiritual one. I sit to commune with this person, with their spirit and soul, as an ancestor who has much to teach me intellectually but also at a spiritual and soul level. I ritualise such practices of reading what I consider sacred texts so that I may open myself up not just at the level of the mind but also the body, spirit, and soul – so that I find my entire being in a space vulnerable and open enough to be changed and transformed through what I read. To connect with the souls of Black folk throughout history and beyond. When I picked up Steve Biko's (1987) *I Write What I Like*, I took it with me to the river each day to sit with the currents as I absorbed this wondrous text. Steve's work changed me forever. It affirmed to me something I had felt for a long time, that the revolution is spiritual and that, without a handle on philosophy and knowledge itself, our struggles are empty and directionless. I recognise the work of Black liberation as connected spiritual work that I intend to continue, through learning from and connecting with those who have gone before as ancestors and spirits who are alive as energies. This is undisciplined scholarly commitment; it is regarding spirituality as epistemology, which, in itself, is leaning into another layer of consciousness.

Francis Fukuyama, an American political scientist, claimed in *The End of History and the Last Man* (2020) that we have come to the end of ideological innovation in the world and that Western Liberal Democracy (WLD) is indeed the end of history. Whilst this work has been critiqued from a number of angles (Hirst, 1989; Badiou, 2012; Milne, 2012; Zhang, 2013;

Gottcke, 2020), its impact, and the climate it reflected, over 30 years on from its first publication, is still vast. The collective ability to imagine beyond Western Liberal Democracy is incredibly limited, to such an extent that much of the focus in terms of work that is done in service of making the world a better place falls within the constraints of WLD. Consider charities, not-for-profits, NGOs – the aim is often to adjust the system from within, to repurpose its resources to people and communities in need, or to focus on one specific injustice within a system that is inherently unjust. Our collective relationship to freedom is deeply fractured; scarcely is the aim of dominant modern movements to transform consciousness, uproot the entire system, and believe another world is possible. This kind of work can often be left to certain realms of the arts and literary fiction; though activists, thinkers, and writers such as adrienne maree brown (2019), Walidah Imarisha (2013), brown and Imarisha (2015), and the indelible Octavia Butler (2019a, 2019b) are, and have been, demonstrating that there is no separation in these worlds. Nothing is more necessary than for us all to recognise ourselves as artists and the creative creators of new worlds – it is the freedom of imagination the artist holds to craft and imagine the world anew and then lead us into drawing that into concrete reality that we must all claim. The artists are the architects of the new world. It is here where fiction and non-fiction find a meeting place to dance and stretch over into one another to recognise that the separation projected onto them was always an illusion. That which is fictitious and considered impossible with ease and grace becomes possible.

There is no shortage of people committed to working towards a better world, but I do believe there is a shortage of imagination to take us to possibilities that exist beyond WLD. Western Liberal Democracy offers a profoundly false promise, and that is the possibility that liberty and freedom can exist within its constraints. In this vein it exploits our deeper knowings, what I would consider soul-level knowings, that freedom and liberation are indeed possible. WLD promises that somewhere along its linear trajectory of progression we will someday meet such freedoms. History is not over; we do not have to work within the impossible restraints of WLD. There is a world beyond democracy, and we may not be able to imagine exactly what that world looks like from where we are standing but that does not mean that such a world is not possible; it just means we must be fearless enough and claim our right to imagine.

Undisciplined offers considerations and a framework for the contemporary consciousness movement that is very much underway. This consciousness movement challenges what is considered freedom. It pushes us to deepen our awareness of the oppressions that are normalised when placed in contrast to what can be perceived as greater unfreedoms such as the dichotomy between the prison and the 'free' world. There is nothing free 'bout the 'free' world. The contemporary consciousness movement reminds us that all knowledge is created, truth is created, what is possible is created. In this vein we can, too, then create knowledges and philosophies that offer us lines of flight out of the constraints of WLD and into different possible worlds. This consciousness movement reminds us that alternative realities, different ways of being, are both possible and necessary. It is a deeply spiritual movement and recognises that all the work begins with the self, but a self connected to community and land. *Undisciplined* gives language and form to some of this consciousness-raising and philosophical work of liberation that is being done in the contemporary world as well as offering ideas on how to deepen this consciousness raising. We explore beyond the materiality of abolition and delve into what philosophies and knowledges we must become conscious of, not only to bring forth new visions of collective freedom, but also to sustain such a world.

Who Are We?

Accordingly, we cannot only fight for the end of the prison and policing systems, or any other institution for that matter; we must fight and struggle too against knowledge itself. When we track epistemological and metaphysical genealogies of the modern world, we find much of its reasoning in Western European Enlightenment thought. These ideas have come to be so broadly held and accepted that they now arguably form the basis of what we might consider common sense. These are ideas about the fundamental and foundational workings of the world that were for a time emergent philosophical ideas fighting to gain legitimacy. In this, we recognise that these ideas can too be reshaped and overthrown as the foundational principles upon which life in the modern world is organised. Different canonical models are possible. One key idea or philosophical principle I will grapple with here is the metaphysical and ethical question of the natural state of human beings. I want you to take a moment and consider what are your core beliefs about your fellow humans? What do you believe about the inherent nature of each person? Are people inherently good? Are some good and some bad? Are all inherently bad? Do we all have some good and bad within us? Do good and bad even exist?

It is upon this assumption that much of the social world we create rests. This is a question philosophers have pondered for centuries, a response to which the emergence of social contract theory offered during the Enlightenment period. Social contract theory is central to the development of the Western European philosophical tradition: it aims to understand how and why we have consented into society as we know it. Within social contract theory the development of the State of Nature offers a conjectural history of humanity before all forms of state apparatus and control were developed such as monarchies, laws, governments, and prisons, and casts an idea of how humanity would have functioned at such a time. Thomas

Hobbes was an English political philosopher who offered us one of the earlier formulations of social contract theory, and arguably one of the most impactful. In *The Leviathan* he imagined the world before the State and rendered it 'solitary, poor, nasty, brutish and short' (Hobbes, 1929 [1651], p. 97), and claimed that the state of nature is a state of war. Essentially making the assertion that all humans are self-seeking and thus require the State and its laws and apparatus to protect us from each other as we would be in a state of constant violence and war, in turn we relinquish some of our freedoms for this State that *should* protect us. This is a foundational principle of liberalism, that human nature is inherently self-seeking and therefore we must organise our world around that. Thomas Hobbes particularly had a deeply pessimistic view of humanity and advocated that only absolute monarchy is a strong enough form of governance to offer social order. So, if we are to believe all humans are inherently bad, then it is important for us to be conscious that this idea is not simply an idea that emerges out of scientific fact but is a philosophical idea that can be shaped and reshaped. What was your response to the earlier questions about the nature of humanity? Some may argue that, in witnessing humanity do evil unto others, it is simply a fact that humans are either inherently bad – or at the very least cannot be inherently good. In response to such a claim, I question what came first – the conditions of scarcity, capital, and harms that create circumstances in which humans carry out acts we may consider 'bad' or the inherence of human evil.

In contrast to the idea that humans are inherently bad, Steve Biko (1987, p. 93) wrote in his essay 'Black consciousness and the quest for true humanity':

> There was no hell in our religion. We believed in the inherent goodness of man – hence we took it for granted that all people at death joined the community of saints and therefore merited our respect. It was the missionaries who confused the people

with their new religion. They scared our people with stories of hell.

Here Steve offers us an alternative conception of the inherent nature of humanity. When considering the relationship between Christianity and European Enlightenment thought, we recognise that the Biblical story of Adam and Eve concerning the 'fall of man' is essentially consistent with the Hobbesian notion of the inherence of human evil. Steve goes on to argue that by 'some strange and twisted logic, they argued theirs [Christianity] was a scientific religion and ours a superstition' (Biko, 1987, p. 93). Further illuminating the relationship between Western European philosophical principles and those of Christian theology – the illusion of the separation between Church and State becomes ever clearer. I would even go as far as to consider the site of the prison as an extension of the philosophy of hell – that only a society and philosophy deeply connected with theologies that consider hell as a possible resting place for souls beyond this lifetime would also consider the prison as a just and necessary aspect of society. The prison is foundationally based on the idea that some people are bad and thus must be punished and corrected; in a similar vein hell is based on the belief that some people live bad lives and so too should be punished for eternity for such transgressions.

So, if we were to perceive all humans as inherently good, what kind of society would we construct to hold such beings? Thomas' philosophy was based on a conjectural history he crafted in his imagination of what humanity may have been like based on his beliefs and subjective viewpoint of society. Thomas was also writing during the context of the English Civil War, which undoubtedly influenced his philosophy. My point, however, is not that we should disregard Thomas Hobbes because of the subjective biases in his philosophy – quite the opposite – we should become conscious of these biases and read his work through them. We must historicise and personalise philosophy – as opposed to considering it as out of the realm of bias and as timeless truths. With this, it is also possible that from this position in which we live and write, we too may be able to imagine alternative histories and futures through our own imaginations which are indeed shaped through the society in which we live and breathe.

We are living in the imagination of men like Thomas Hobbes; imagination is not a scarce resource. We all must claim our right to imagine and then do the philosophical work of both challenging and creating knowledge and epistemologies that serve in supporting how we might remake the world in the wake of philosophical standpoints that may no longer serve. We live in a world underwritten by fear: the social contract dictates that we have either explicitly or tacitly expunged some of our freedom in order to maintain social order and keep ourselves safe. When we consider the way the State treats Black life, we immediately recognise that social order and safety are far from what the State offers. Thomas offered a conjectural history – we too can sculpt and craft conjectural futures through our imaginations and create worlds that are entirely different. It is a shift in consciousness that is required to recognise the illegitimacy of the presiding knowledge system as the sole author of truth and recognise that alternative knowledge systems can, and must, be created.

Movement Towards Freedom

When I first heard someone call the work of activism 'movement work' I was sold. What a beautiful use of layered and textured language that offers meaning to the work we are doing. Motion, movement, change. 'Movement' honours what the prolific science and speculative fiction writer Octavia Butler (2019a) referred to as 'the only lasting truth' (p. 3) and that is change. Movement does not suggest we are working in one single direction, or even that our aims are the same, but it instead honours the aliveness of the work we are doing. That we are always in motion, moving with the winds and tides of change. When I look to nature, I am reminded that everything is always in motion, in movement. Even if my naked eye cannot observe the loving dance of photosynthesis the plants do each day with the sun in the sky, I know and I trust that it is happening. Nature is always in movement, from the leaves jostling in the wind, to waters speaking at the mouth of the stream, right down to the cellular level of the wonders of plant microbiology. So too are we always in movement. The world is ever changing and whether that change is just moving deeper into different formulations of Western Liberal Democracy, moving into authoritarian regimes, or into other possibilities that are yet to be touched by humanity in the modern world is up to us. Octavia Butler (2019a) reminds us that we can and we must 'shape the universe' (p. 74), change and movement is inevitable, but we have the power to shape that change into what we imagine the world should be, and this is achieved through intentional movements towards freedom. We are in movement because we are alive.

I have been a part of movements across the world such as Black Lives Matter UK and Decolonising the University, movements that strive towards us all getting free. Through this I have come to recognise that much of the focus and efforts of such radical movements is making change within the material world. What I mean by this is that these movements are often focused on the level of life, how we might make immediate changes to make life more liveable – whether that is to change curricula or university processes, or to influence the criminal justice and policing systems to keep our people alive. This work is incredibly important and central to the movement work that is necessary to take us into new worlds, but it is only one part of the story.

In recent years I have come to question more and more whether through this activism and the meeting of such demands, will freedom truly encounter us on the other side? I often think when one demand is met, we will only become more aware of the unending unfreedoms we are subjected to in its wake. One win based on our demands becomes less so a gateway to freedom, and more so a portal to understanding the truer extent of just how unfree we are. This, however, is necessary because it is a core part of the consciousness-raising work, though when not seen through this lens these events serve more as an offering of overwhelm or defeat, as opposed to a gateway to understanding the necessity of new worlds and how me might attain such worlds. Still, movement work cannot only be carried out at the material level and cannot be about only changing the systems we are living within. We must also be very serious about the destruction of these systems, not just in rhetoric but also in developing philosophies and knowledges that ground a world beyond such systems.

As such, I have come to understand the question of freedom and liberation as less so questions that can be answered solely at the level of material action. This is because our material reality of unfreedom is based on an epistemology, a knowledge system, that upholds such harm and unfreedom as the norm. If we are not to challenge the knowledge system itself from its root and foundations, the material action will lack the imagination and direction necessary to truly transform our world. With this, I felt my activism was trapped in a cycle of challenging the *expressions* of a harmful and unjust system, as opposed to its core. I recognised that this alone would never bring about the liberation I desired to see. To get free, we must challenge the immaterial and take on the question of transforming the epistemology that grounds the entire system. Ironically, the increased focus on material and measurable change within radical movements is a reflection of a knowledge system itself that values empiricism, change that can be experienced in a measurable and concrete way, over other forms of knowledge. How do we define and evaluate our movements outside of this empiricist philosophy of impact mapping and productivity? To move towards freedom and liberation we must challenge the knowledge system itself. This means exploring the immaterial and all that upholds these knowledge systems that legitimise harm. We must transform our relationship to knowledge itself if we are to draw up lines of flight that move us into new worlds of abolition where a continual cycle of struggle and fighting is no longer the reality for people at the margins. Instead, liberation just simply *is*.

In the introduction to Stefano Harney and Fred Moten's (2013) *The Undercommons: Fugitive Planning & Black Study*, it is posed that what Frantz Fanon was actually striving towards through his work was 'not the end of colonialism but the end of the standpoint from which colonialism makes sense' (p. 8). This is a reflection on knowledge, or epistemology: it is argued that Frantz was more interested in how colonialism was produced as an idea, and how such an idea was validated and consequently produced and reproduced as legitimate. Thus, what are the epistemological foundations that allow all the harms and ills of society to make sense? In this vein, *Undisciplined* takes on this question and sets about unpicking and undoing the logics upon which our modern society rests to understand how we might be able to re-envision societal harms as illegitimate and non-sensical. Injustices, prison systems, harmful institutions make sense and are continually validated and reproduced because of the epistemological consensus of the modern world. So, what might it take for such injustices to cease to make sense?

Abolition is the demand for a new world, for new beginnings in the wake of oppressive and harmful systems. When referring to new worlds, I take the concept of 'world' as an epistemological location as opposed to a physical one. Throughout *Undisciplined*, we will explore how we might transform our relationship to knowledge itself in the pursuit of liberation for all. *Undisciplined* takes the University to be the centre-point of knowledge production in the modern world; that is to say, if something is not in some way or at some stage validated through the University, it is discarded as fiction or speculation. As such, knowledges and belief systems of indigenous peoples have been relegated to the realms of untruth in favour of knowledges that are grounded in, and can be validated by, the scientific method.

So, what might it take to remove the university as the centre point of knowledge production in the modern world? What possibilities does this offer for liberation and the expansion of what is possible? *Undisciplined* shifts the focal location of abolition away from the prison and towards the university. To explore the ways that our minds, emotions, spirits, and souls have been disciplined by the education system at large, and the level of consciousness it teaches, the foundation of this system is at the heart of the university. Still, as aforementioned with regard to the prison, the university is also used here as a mechanism to speak through when considering abolition, the whole of society as we know it must be abolished and built anew. We could hold this conversation from various starting points such as the school system, though the school system is designed by those that have been educated in the university from curriculum design to institutional organisation. So, I hold that the university is a pertinent location for us to think through and consider what its abolition may offer. We must break out of the confines and limitations that the university has placed on knowledge and our minds, and by extension all forms of institutionalised education. We must imagine anew what we fundamentally believe is possible and, with this, how we might shape our world and collective futures.

The Decolonial Question

Why Is My Curriculum White?
Rhodes Must Fall.
Why Isn't My Professor Black?

I was an undergraduate during the time that the contemporary student decolonial movement was at its peak – this peak, I would argue, was from around 2013 until 2017. I cannot mention these movements without mentioning my dear friend and comrade Nathaniel Tobias ~~Coleman~~ – an insurgent intellectual whose work across the UK, with all of the listed movements, ignited my critical decolonial journey in the academy. I came across these movements at the same time I began to feel deeply dissatisfied with the curriculum on my own degree. I would often share that it felt I had to almost 'forget' things I knew to be true in my own life in order to pass my highly analytical philosophy degree. Knowledge produced by those outside of the white male able norm as discarded as having no place in the analytics of philosophy. For the entire philosophy side of my degree, we did not read a single person who was not white. I was not taught by a single person who was not white. I was even told by a lecturer that around two Black women (at the time I identified as a Black woman) began the degree each year and they always tended to struggle and not complete. He wanted to understand how I was achieving decent grades and progressing year to year. I had nothing to say to him. The course was not designed for people like me to succeed; it required us to leave ourselves at the door and embrace harmful reductionist thinking as unchallengeable truth and pretend like the philosophers we were reading were not also the architects of racism as we know it. Mentally and emotionally the degree was a location of pain.

So, when I first discovered these radical movements challenging the university and curriculum design, I immediately felt a deep resonance. There was a revolutionary fervour in the air, the social media site Facebook was increasingly popular at the time, and this is where I began to find information and community to discuss these radical movements. Students all over the world were coming together and engaging in radical discourse about the state of the university with the recognition that change was both necessary and possible, and that we could all play a part in bringing forth such change.

Since then, I have been a proponent of decolonial work, firstly taking on my own university and then supporting decolonial movements at universities across the UK and internationally. I was elected as a Students Union Sabbatical Officer for two years, 2015–2017, and I spent these two years focused on decolonising the university and supporting marginalised students. Alongside my activism I was studying decolonial thought and trying to bring decolonial theory into practice. I came to recognise that the closer I got to the machine of the university, the more impossible decolonial dreams felt. The bureaucracy, the resistance, and the shame I witnessed come up for those at the centre of the university felt insurmountable at times. Eventually, the decolonial work became relegated to some working group at the fringes of the university and I believe this to be true for a number of movements across the UK and across the world. The institution would do just enough to demonstrate that it was 'doing the work', but protect the university from any systemic challenges made by the decolonial demand.

I began to question whether the university could actually be decolonised. I spent many years dedicated to this work of 'decolonising the university' alongside many powerful comrades, believing it was possible within our lifetimes if we fought hard enough. I still believe decoloniality is possible in my lifetime, and that is because I recognise it already exists in so many spaces and communities outside of the university. Decoloniality is here; it just eludes the university. By extension, I have come to believe that the university cannot be decolonised.

Instead, to decolonise the university means to abolish it.

This is because coloniality is the foundation of the university; if coloniality were to be removed from the university the university would cease to exist. This is how interrelated and interdependent coloniality and the university are. If we agree that the university should be decolonised if it is to be legitimate, then the university must be abolished because it cannot be decolonised. This was a tough pill to swallow as in part it rendered years of my life and energy as futile; I was dedicated to this movement with every bone in my body. Still, I would not have come to recognise that the university cannot be decolonised had I not struggled inside the heart of the movement. With this, I chose to divest from the institution with regard to my activism, the university is obsolete, and so I began thinking through what university abolition may look like.

Still, the only place where decoloniality began to feel marginally possible was in my personal academic and intellectual work, as opposed to the institution at large, so I continued the pursuit of gaining greater understanding of decolonial technologies and possibilities into my master's studies and beyond. It was an art I had to skill myself up in to say what I truly wanted to say but still toe the institutional disciplinary lines and boundaries. This is because if I had fully embraced the decolonial question, I may not have passed my degrees as the conclusions the exploration led me to would not have been validated within the academy. This work further cemented for me that the university cannot be decolonised, and so the strategy for the radical work must be different.

I also saw the grave injustices of looking around at my comrades in the movement and at my own personal life and recognising that we were all exhausted and dangerously burnt out. That we had continually taken on the additional, often unpaid, labour of striving towards decoloniality within our institutions. In turn we saw the institutions benefitting from appearing to engage in 'decolonial' work whilst the students at the helm of such work, and their degrees, suffered. It felt counter-productive, that we must spend all of our energy struggling within the institution to simply have an education that isn't oppressive whilst our less marginalised counterparts could unassumingly enjoy their degrees. I divested from the university, and I have also divested from a paradigm of activism that legitimises and even glorifies *struggle*. The mechanisms and strategies we use to shape the change we long to see must embody the change we are collectively trying to bring about. Marginalised students over-working whilst gaining significant debt for degrees that are inherently colonial is not a struggle I can any longer be a part of. What does it look like to organise in a way that welcomes the ease and justice we are aiming to realise?

Still, whilst I fundamentally believe the university is obsolete and I have divested from the institution in terms of my activism, I write this book whilst enrolled as a PhD researcher at the University of Cambridge. A contradiction indeed. But this is what Stefano Harney and Fred Moten (2013) describe as a 'fugitive manoeuvre', being *at* the university in order to utilise its resources but not *of* the university. What possibilities exist at the borders of the institution where we might repatriate its resources into consciousness-raising work that is in service of liberation, and no longer look towards the university itself as a site of possibility, and instead as a site of probable demise? This is the foundation of Undisciplined Scholarly Commitment.

2

The Undisciplined Embodied

There is a certain grace within intellectual work, particularly in research, where one is given the opportunity to explore, with little restriction, wherever inquiry takes them. It is through this kind of intellectual work I have come to define my relationship more clearly to the university, and my relationship to myself. It is with this that we may begin to consider how we might harness what is salvageable within the university to move us closer to freedom and liberation. To make clear, the machine of the university and the epistemic base of the university's validation processes are inherently colonial, though what may be encountered in the process of *study* itself and exploration offers possible freedoms and opportunities for expansion beyond the colonial knowledge system.

Critical Black feminist intellectual bell hooks (1994, p. 59) wrote, in *Teaching to Transgress*:

> I came to theory because I was hurting – the pain within me was so intense that I could not go on living. I came to theory desperate, wanting to comprehend – to grasp what was happening around and within me. Most importantly, I wanted to make the hurt go away. I saw in theory then a location of healing.

Theory and intellectual work have healed me many times over; they have offered me language and frameworks to understand life and experiences that have at times felt too large to comprehend. For me, this is the power of intellectual and academic work – to delve into unknown realms, make sense, and offer language to that which before had been experienced but not understood. This is true from the sciences to the social sciences, and so I want to make clear that *Undisciplined* is not a pursuit of anti-intellectualism; it is quite the opposite. *Undisciplined* is about challenging what is considered common sense and bringing about consciousness surrounding the presiding knowledge system that governs our world. To be Undisciplined is to engage in this epistemic refusal of this notion and name the knowledge system at play. In this vein we are able to transform both our relationship to the knowledge system *and* the knowledge system itself through intentional and radical approaches to shaping epistemologies.

The Undisciplined Scholar is a heuristic device I offer here to think through how those of us who occupy space within the university may utilise such space to bring about the freedom dream of liberation and other possible worlds. How do we occupy the borders of the institution and make the goal of our intellectual work not just the theorisation of freedom but instead the actualisation of it? How do we shatter the boundaries of intellectual inquiry the university has erected, and deepen our pursuit of knowledge beyond its boundaries? What is required from us, especially that which may not be comfortable, to move more deeply into decoloniality?

I recognise that there is something very dangerous happening within the academy. Specifically in the arts and social sciences there is a dislocation between what is being researched and its real-world impact. For instance, a great deal has been written about decoloniality (Bhambra, Gebrial, and Nişancıoğlu, 2018; Kwoba, Chantiluke, and Nkopo, 2018; Du Plessis, 2021; Guzmán Valenzuela, 2021); however, the university is still fundamentally colonised with little to indicate that much will be transformed. Why is this work not rupturing the very foundation of the institution, but instead being subsumed by it? It invokes the question as to whether such intellectual pursuits are being used as just that, intellectual pursuits that, rather than challenge the university, instead reinforce its dominance. I am curious as to why decoloniality has become so sanitised that universities recognise it as both safe and even advantageous to their institutional design to have courses in decolonial thought on the curriculum. As such, the discourse of decoloniality that is intended to resist coloniality in turn becomes hegemonic – it is institutionalised as another discipline within the colonial academy, deradicalising the possibilities and potentialities of decolonial work. I question myself as to whether this is what I was really fighting for.

We find ourselves in a unique place where we have a very attractive and therefore exploitable movement – if we are not careful our work may come to both uphold and legitimise the same colonising forces that we argue we are rejecting. The neoliberal machine of the university requires academics to make work that attracts funding, attracts students, and work that helps support their careers in progressing within the academy to higher-paying roles. Academic and intellectual work has become a market in many ways. I find myself concerned when this relates to radical work because the capacity to challenge the university, or any other institution, to the point of challenging one's own position in the reproduction of its harms is limited. I try to reflect on this constantly through my own academic work and recognise the difficulty and very personal costs of challenging one's own position and career as an aspect of the theoretical work one undertakes; though I believe this is essential if we are serious about getting free.

I have resolved in my own life to write out of the academy instead of into it. The university does not exist in its current form in my speculation of freedom and the possible, and so with good conscience I cannot continue to legitimise its place in the world. It is for this reason I offer the notion of university abolition. Still, this is not to say that whatever I do choose to write into and give my labour towards does not have its own complicated colonial and harmful history – that is very much the cost of living and working under capitalism. However, engaging this with a level of consciousness and self-reflexivity is important, especially when we espouse ideas that hold radical potential. Clearly understanding within ourselves, and when necessary stating, our limitations, complexities, and at times contradictory manoeuvres is paramount to the radical work. This is in service of the transformation we seek, to accept that, and therefore write into the fact, none of us are linear, nor are we without grave contradictions. That is the occupation of being human. Though we live within a knowledge system that uplifts simplicity and clear definitions, and rejects the chaos (read: truth) of what it means to live complex lives. A lack of linearity in our work is not something we should reject – it is something to be embraced, considered, and expounded upon.

When it comes to how I can engage with the university in lieu of its abolition, I look to the generous work of Stefano Harney and Fred Moten (2013) in *The Undercommons: Fugitive Planning & Black Study*, who offer us the conception of the subversive intellectual as a potential maroon community of scholars who are 'unprofessional, uncollegial, passionate and disloyal' (p. 10). The main aim of such a community is to steal from the institution and 'abuse its hospitality, to spite its mission, to join its refugee colony, its gypsy encampment, to be in but not of' (p. 26). This offering of fugitive intellectualism, wherein the intellectual disappears into what Stefano and Fred call the *undercommons of enlightenment*, to do the radical and subversive work is an important offering to understanding the potential of different fugitive manoeuvres one can make within the university. My own experience speaks to the nature of the subversive intellectual, in that I regard my place at

Cambridge as one from which I am at an institution abundant with resources, and in receipt of a full scholarship, but I do not see myself as in service of the university. Rather, I see myself as a conduit through which the resources of the university can be extended back into the communities I serve. I strive to achieve this through following a road of intellectualism that deprioritises the institution and instead priorities freedom and liberation for all.

Whilst the Undisciplined Scholar holds these foundational beliefs, the concept is less about *how* one does the work of radical intellectualism and more about *who* one is, and who one must become, to embody the fervent mission of creating the world anew. Importantly, the locus of focus is within the self, not on creating change in the external world as either dislocated from the self or outside of the self – this will be expanded upon below. The concept of the Undisciplined Scholar arises from my own experience of engaging in decolonial, activist, and intellectual work to challenge the academy as well as other institutions such as the police and the government. It arises from beautiful and powerful elements in the many people I have met on this journey and those comrades I have worked and visioned alongside in the aim to create a better world. It arises from those I met through my travels engaging in decolonial and liberation work across Europe, South Africa, Brazil, and the United States, and the many more comrades I met through engaging in radical and care-based work in online spaces. To each person that has inspired this work, I thank you.

The Undisciplined Scholar is a radical intellectual, who often embodies the nature of the subversive intellectual as defined by Stefano and Fred. Though each negotiates their role and capacity in a way that most closely aligns with their unique offerings to the movement, not all are in the *undercommons of enlightenment*. There is no one single way to take on the institution; we must remain agile and adaptable in movements for liberation, and so defining *what* such radicals should do can be counterproductive to the goal of developing multiple and boundless lines of flight into new worlds. Whilst the Undisciplined Scholar is located specifically at the university, this kind of work can be applied in any institution as creating lines of flight in the realm of knowledge and embodiment is necessary in every field. I will now define some elements of who the Undisciplined Scholar is through *intention, identity,* and *action.*

Intention

Intention is often a faculty that is disregarded in the modern world, omitted in favour of 'impact' or 'evidence-based' results. This mode of valuing approaches is broadly considered as common-sense – organisations work towards their key performance indicators, impact mapping, and quantifying measurable change. When we consider organisational changemaking, movements for justice, and arguably even in our personal lives, that which is measurable and quantifiable takes precedence over whatever intention was placed behind what has been created. I want to shift the perspective around this and argue that intention is just as important as impact.

The intention of the Undisciplined Scholar is where the radical work begins; without this foundation nothing can be achieved in the material world, nothing of consequence. Intention begins in the heart space, a space of desire and expansion – it is in the heart space the desire and knowing of the possibility of another world is instigated. Intention forms the foundation of the movement. The movement for liberation and creating new worlds is not a movement for which we can rely upon historic data to show us what steps should be taken to achieve the goals we seek. This is not to say that there is not a pantheon of radical workers and movements throughout history for us to look back upon and learn from – as we must always invoke the Akan proverb of Sankofa (go back and get it) as a grounding principle of the work we do – though it is to say that no historical community has faced and navigated through the precise challenges we face today in the technological world in which we live. Every move to liberation is opening a portal into another world; our ancestors guided us to the freedoms we experience today as comparable to times of lesser freedoms, but it is incumbent on us to both redefine what freedom and liberation looks like today, as well as open that portal to allow those that come after us to walk into freedoms we were unable to experience in our lifetimes. This is also not to suggest that 'progress' of this work is in any way linear, and because of this, intention is ever more important and central to the welcoming in of new worlds.

So, evidence-based strategies become limited because this is unprecedented territory in the modern world when the aims of the work, creating new worlds and possibilities, are honoured in full and not censored or shrunk. As such, the work of movement is messy and complicated. However, when the impact of the work is counterproductive or harm is caused, it should be rectified and learnt from – I fundamentally believe that this messiness is central to building new worlds. There is no road map or blueprint, and as deeply flawed humans occupying a deeply flawed world, the impact of such noble pursuits may at times run off course, though this does not delegitimise the work itself. The aim to create certainty and clarity through evidence-based approaches or through looking at the external world through impact, curbs the creativity and possibilities of radical work. The road to freedom is not linear, and we should not try to make it so. Leaning into the mess that working from a space of intention may create allows us to shape greater possibilities through honouring the multiple roads to freedom and liberation that may be shaped and created.

Hence, intention is central. Whilst we cannot evaluate the intentions and hearts of others, we must lean into realms we are taught to fear, such as trust. Intention is created in the realm of the unseen, it cannot be 'objectively' analysed and measured in a way that can be validated by a systemised process and then gain legitimacy in our current epistemological model of truth. As such, this devaluation of intention is again an inflection of the knowledge system that believes that which happens in the material world and can be observed by others is more important than what happens in unseen realms. The Undisciplined Scholar embodies a knowledge system they long to see and welcomes the dangerous road of trust and uncertainty it may invoke. The Undisciplined Scholar welcomes the reality that none of us knows exactly how we are going to move towards freedom, which, as discussed above, is undefinable. There is little evidence and no assured path we can all look towards. That the road to liberation is a dislocated collection of radical experiments taking place for which the only connecting principle is the desire for freedom and liberation.

So, by way of intention and belief system, the Undisciplined Scholar is a beacon of hope, a believer in the possibility of the unseen, a believer in the idea that another world is possible. They are a believer in the pursuit of radical study as a route to liberation, a believer in the power and ability of knowledge production, with its limits inside the academy, and recognise it as limitless outside of the academy. The Undisciplined Scholar rejects rationality and empiricism as the only valid routes to knowing – they engage and seek out alternative ways of knowing, sometimes that they bring to the academy and sometimes that they simply experience in their personal life. This is key because the Undisciplined Scholar who is committed to liberation knows that we must challenge the very knowledge system that upholds society, not just the results and expressions of this knowledge system.

They also recognise that the first system they must revolutionise is that within the self, they recognise that the radical work cannot be done without consistent renewal and healing within their own life and heart. The Undisciplined Scholar holds that self and collective healing is an uncompromisable part of the movement to ensure that their own intentions derive from a space of healing and personal and collective care. The Undisciplined Scholar desires freedom and liberation above all; they do not know exactly how to get there but they are resolute in their commitment to put their best foot forward and transform the systems they experience as harmful and unjust. They look over at their comrades doing the work in a way that may not completely resonate with them, but rather than trying to homogenise the movement they trust that intentions are in the right place. With humility and trust they recognise there are many routes to liberation and their own is not superior to another's, though still they stay in skilful and generative conversation and discourse with their comrades and learn what is necessary for collective and strategic moves to further the cause of liberation. They remain agile and adaptable, returning continually to their heart space in recognition that this is where the freedom dream begins, and where the knowledge of how best to navigate closer to that freedom dream emanates from.

Identity

Those that have inspired this concept of the Undisciplined Scholar have all held identities that exist at the margins, and that is because from this space the requirement to disrupt, as an act of survival within the academy, can be present. These identities may lie at the lines of race, ability, neurodiversity, gender, and so on. Whilst I do believe anyone can be an Undisciplined Scholar, our relationship to ourselves and our own identities cannot be overlooked. It is from my identity that my personal political and movement work began. I recognised that I was treated differently based on my race and gender and decided that I would do my best to make a stand against this. As time went on, I was introduced to Black Feminist Theory at university, and this transformed the trajectory of my life in a powerful and unwavering way. I read the Combahee River Collective Statement as part of an elective module I took convened by Professor Shirley Ann Tate on race, feminism, and culture in the School of Sociology at the University of Leeds. I say her name, Professor Shirley Ann Tate, because as the only Black woman I was taught by throughout my undergraduate and master's degrees, her presence and offering transformed my life and my trajectory of study. It is important to note and make clear that I had to take a module outside of my chosen degree programme (Philosophy and Politics) to experience such a lecturer and to experience this dimension of knowledge.

The Combahee River Collective Statement, written by queer working-class Black women in 1977, offered me language and a sense of community even though I did not know these women from across the Atlantic, but, as a Black British 20-year-old woman-identified person (at the time), I saw myself in their words. It is credited as a key early articulation of intersectional Black feminist thinking, and is a powerful reflection-cum-manifesto of the experience of Black womanhood in the United States. This is when the healing that theory offers began for me. Whilst Black feminism had consistently been present throughout my life and in my relationships, the way these women offered language and analysis of the systems and our identities brought a sense of peace and resonance that is beyond words. It was with the language and analysis of social conditions that Black feminism offered that I was able to step into a more unapologetic season of my radical work. I was able to specifically understand a genealogy of the oppressions that I was experiencing and in turn I was able to challenge them in more intelligible ways. Hence, the Undisciplined Scholar is a seeker of the knowledge of their own conditions, not necessarily for the sake of activism or any action, but for the process of healing and developing in consciousness. This was exactly what Black feminist thought has done for me – it was a complete shift in consciousness that opened up new possibilities and new routes to healing, understanding, and accepting myself.

The Combahee River Collective Statement, and much of the identity politics work that came after it, offered an important analysis of how oppressive systems interrelatedly work and form our complex experiences of harmful structures in society. The Undisciplined Scholar understands and acknowledges this, but they also recognise and theorise about their identity as a site of possibility, not only as a location through which to understand oppression. In my own life I have come to shift from understanding identity primarily through the lens of oppression to understanding identity as the foundation of my relationship to the possible.

My body is undisciplined. I take my lessons on what is possible through the canvas of my own body and the iterations, reformulations, and transformations my identity and physical form have expanded through in this lifetime. As a transgender person, I have witnessed myself be made anew. There is much to say about the oppressions myself and all transgender people face in this world, but I must highlight that nothing has shaped my relationship to the possible as much as my experience of gender and my ability to transform myself. My gender is a site of possibility. When many of us come into this world, we are told who we are; our identities are essentially given to us. Gender is offered as a static unchangeable principle of identity when you enter this world – that child is either a boy or a girl. This is often considered as a simple fact. Trans people play artfully with the possible each day; we take what many of us were told was impossible to change as children and run amuck with it. We open doors we were told did not even exist. We artfully gallop beyond the thresholds of mind, body, spirit, and soul and access knowings within ourselves that are beyond measurability and comprehension outside of ourselves. We become our own authority and must trust the knowledge we hold of our own identity over whatever the world may want to tell us. We become us.

My identity has taught me that the unimaginable is imaginable. That the impossible is both possible but also necessary. That life only has the limits we place upon it. My body and my identity are unruly, undisciplined, play to no conventions. In the article 'Cultivating the scavenger: a queerer feminist future for composition and rhetoric', Stacey Waite explores the possibilities of queer methodologies. Stacy focuses on Jack Halberstam's (2018) notion of queer scavenger methodologies, which suggests the art of queering methodologies includes bringing together disparate methods that may appear at times at odds to form methodology. Stacey Waite (2015, p. 15) offers a beautiful articulation of this approach and their own experience:

> My body is not coherent. One might say, for example, 'This is not a girl' or 'This is not a boy.' My trajectory as a writer is also incoherent . . . what is so queer about this scavenging, about refusing coherence, about combining that which seems separate or seemingly unrelated.

My body too is incoherent; I now live my life as an almost exclusively male-assumed person. Assumptions are made about my body that are simply inconsistent with my own experience of my body. If people were to uncloak the layers that adorn me each day, they would find a beautifully uncompromisingly undisciplined body. A body that plays to no conventions in a cisgendered and phallogocentric world. There is an intimate relationship between an undisciplined body and the rejection of the disciplined belief and commitment to the institution. Undisciplined bodies come in all shapes, sizes, abilities, races, and any other formulation that is inconsistent with the dominant narrative of the body. The university was not designed to, and as such the university does not know how to, hold such bodies and identities. I feel myself spilling out over its boundaries, even in the times I wanted nothing more than to shrink myself to remain within its limits. To spill out wasn't a choice. Though it is a process I honour and have decided to no longer work against the current of. I believe I have no choice but to write out of the institution because I will never be fully embraced by the institution. Either I dishonour myself and my own identity or I dishonour the institution. To honour oneself and acknowledge the possibilities one's identity offers them to shape lines of flight beyond the confines of the institution is undisciplined scholarly commitment, no matter the costs.

Action

By way of action the Undisciplined Scholar is a mover and shaker. They recognise that the work cannot be intellectual nor spiritual or heart-based alone; they recognise that the work must be brought into tangible reality and so they develop the necessary skills to see this through. The aim of the Undisciplined Scholar is to vision alternative ways of being and new realities; they engage in the work of radical imagination internally within self and co-create visions collectively. The imagination is the womb space of creation and possibility, and they recognise that this is the foundation of any action that can be taken, for without depth and expanse of imagination, we simply recreate the same limiting and constricting world we already inhabit. The Undisciplined Scholar then aims to create a rope and anchor long and light enough to spin and throttle into the heavens of their imagination so that they might anchor on to their freedom dreams and pull by pull anchor that dream into concrete reality. They are the co-creators of new worlds.

The action the Undisciplined Scholar takes has many and infinite forms. They move in action towards where their imagination and heart space leads, and therefore the possibility of what their work may look like is limitless. Importantly, the Undisciplined Scholar does not wait for perfection nor a water-tight hypothesis to move into taking action on what they believe will lead to new pastures of liberation. They recognise that *movement* is necessary to see perspectives they were not privy to at each entrance point to radical work. In this, the more action they take the more becomes possible because the space to shed confusion and experiment with their speculations is possible. The introduction to Stefano Harney and Fred Moten's (2013, p. 6) aforementioned work offers an important acknowledgement in that

> we cannot say what new structures will replace the ones we live with yet, because once we have torn shit down, we will inevitably see more and see differently and feel a new sense of wanting and being and becoming. What we want after 'the break' will be different from what we think we want before the break.

As mentioned, no one knows what a clear road to liberation looks like. The vantage point from which we engage in this work is limited to the world in which we live – it is inconsistent with the expansiveness of the goals of liberation to expect ourselves to have a clear and concise road map of our collective freedom dreams. Action is therefore pivotal. The Undisciplined Scholar engages in an alluring composition of radical experiments to engage in the process of moving towards liberation, albeit in a nonlinear and ever-changing way. Actions may expand, and then contract and contort even more, to then expand again. In this vein, we must 'tear shit down' so that we can see the treasure, or simply dispose of the waste, that lies in the ruins of this world. To see what lies beyond those ruins. What flowers or crops may grow in its place when we liberate the fertile soil from the archaic institutions that have been weighing it down?

To borrow from movement visionary and facilitator adrienne maree brown's (2017) work in *Emergent Strategy*, the Undisciplined Scholar is adaptable. They accept that change is inevitable, as mentioned, and so as such they must become adaptable to the ever-changing world and circumstances they find themselves in. They are rigorous in learning and understanding and then embodying the change they long to see. Step by step, experiment by experiment, they aim to sharpen and better execute their action towards their freedom dreams and recognise adaptability as a uncompromisable element of this work.

They are also the planter of radical seeds within the minds and hearts of all they engage with. They recognise that action is never a lone enterprise, nor is it one that can or must only happen in immediate structured community. The Undisciplined Scholar recognises that for any sustained change to take place there must be sprouts of radical work occupying all corners of the Earth and that they are a small part of a wider ecosystem of world transformation. In this way, they see planting a radical seed of possibility through words or actions that may not come to any material consequence – but have affected the hearts or minds of others as just as much a radical action as any other. There is no monopoly over radical action; we have more chance of getting free if each of us takes that freedom dream into our own hands. I was radicalised through these kinds of intentional strategic moves by academics, students, and activists who planted radical seeds within me that were able to spark questions that led me to find a new sense of liberation. Still, the Undisciplined Scholar does not look to anyone else to get them free. They see their own divine right to shape and orchestrate change in community and connection as their guiding force towards a new world. They wait for no one to offer them permission or legitimacy. They see the divine in themselves, just as they see the divine in others, and it is through this divinity that they recognise that power exists within them to untold degrees. It is a reflection of the ancient Sanskrit greeting 'Namaste', which can be translated as *the divine in me bows to the divine in you.*

3

Disciplining Knowledge

On Discipline

5:00am: Wake up, brush teeth.

5:05am: Boil the kettle, cut a slice of lemon, pour water over the lemon, and take a seat to sip it down.

5:10am: Open my journal and note down what I can remember from the dreams I have just awoken from, exploring the medicine and messages that may be within them to support my daily life.

5:20am: Turn to my right and greet my ancestors a good morning at the altar I have laid for them. Light a candle, offer my gratitude, and pray over the day ahead.

5:30am: Stretch out my body, bringing my head as close to the ground as I can. Deep breathing exercises, ensuring the out breath always lasts longer than the in.

5:40am: Make my morning coffee and sit to speak a list of affirmations over my life.

5:50am: Head to the mirror to witness myself, pump three squirts of testosterone into my hands, and lather them on

each shoulder (it is quite a marvel to remember each day that I can bend the world as I continue to transform myself into something I was taught was impossible).
  6:00am: Take a seat at my desk to begin the daily discipline of writing the worlds that live inside of me into being.
  9:00am: Finish writing and attend to a morning walk along the seafront.

Whilst this book is titled *Undisciplined*, I do not want to deceive you into believing that discipline and routine are not the routes through which it has come into being. Above is my daily timetable, which makes the commitments I aim to meet in my life such as authoring this work possible; I write each morning of the week for at least three hours. This is a discipline that has taken me many years to reach and at times I still fall short, but it remains my optimum framework for both productivity and for happiness. If I were to throw out discipline altogether, I am certain I would be an incredibly unhappy and lost person. Discipline offers us routine and regulation that is supportive to our nervous systems; it also gives us a framework to protect time so that we might be able to form our own expression in the world which can be a profoundly fulfilling and nourishing enterprise.

The argument of *Undisciplined* is not to offer a wholesale rejection of discipline; it is rather to understand the ways that discipline has been used to curb our imagination and faculties of radical and world-bending thought. Michel Foucault (2020) offers a genealogy of the emergence of disciplinary technologies of power across Europe in his seminal work *Discipline and Punish*. He tracks this history from the use of public execution as a spectacle to discipline the masses, to the diffusion of disciplinary power to the point that no one individual enforces power; instead it operates in a way that is 'visible' yet 'unverifiable'. Michel argues that discipline creates docile bodies, 'a body is docile that may be subjected, used, transformed and improved' (p. 136). To become a docile body is to lose agency and succumb to the demand of the technology of disciplinarity on the body. This is enacted through various means, one of which is the 'control of activity' which Michel argues can be found in the common *timetable*. I offer my own timetable above to demonstrate that I believe there are two distinct functions of disciplinarity – that which comes from the self and that which comes from the external system. This of course presupposes there is a self that exists at least somewhat independently of the system, and a complex metaphysical and psychoanalytical discussion concerning mind, body, and soul as to what this self is made up of. Whilst I will not define what I understand as the self here, it is an ever-moving concept that we will continue to explore throughout the text. Still, we will work with the assumption that a self can exist separately and develop thought and action independent of the system, though this self is complex and multiplicitous.

Whilst discipline can create docile bodies when it comes from an externalised system that holds the intention of power over us, it too has the ability to create focused and radical bodies and minds when it derives from the self. Resisting the system in and of itself is a discipline, to hold the boundaries and to consistently remind oneself that the subtle and diffuse power Michel describes is something we can and must mentally circumvent. As the radical and visionary abolitionist Mariame Kaba (2021) puts it, 'hope is a discipline' (p. 27).

As such, navigating spaces of higher education, where the colonial curriculum is the norm, has continued to require a discipline in remaining steadfast to the rejection of coloniality and the demand of more for my own education and that of others. The desire to assimilate can be tantalising at times – it holds a false veneer of peace in which we can rest because we are not fighting the system, but this is in fact docility taking hold. It is the characterisation of the external discipline of institutions, which thrive on our docility. There is great discipline in rejection and in revolution. This is in the same way that to learn to love and maintain love is a conscious discipline, in a world so bereft of love as bell hooks (2018) teaches us in *All About Love: New Visions*. When I look upon the lives and lived experiences of those who I admire for their creative offerings to the world, discipline and structure in their days was always of primacy. For example, speculative fiction writer Octavia Butler rose up between 3am and 4am to begin her daily discipline of writing worlds into words. She found the morning hours before the noise of the world began to be her best writing hours (Currey, 2019). Equally, by the point in her career Toni Morrison was able to be a full-time writer, she rose at 5am each morning. To tend to her discipline of writing, she said, 'writers all devise ways to approach that place where they expect to make the contact, where they become the conduit, or where they engage in this mysterious process'. 'For me, light is the signal in the transaction. It's not being in the light, it's being there before it arrives. It enables me, in some sense' (Morrison cited in Currey, 2020). So, it is important to not view discipline itself as a political arena in which we must take sides to be either entirely disciplined or entirely undisciplined in the traditional sense. A lack of discipline entirely is what leads to docility. The Undisciplining that I am offering as a heuristic in this text is a form that requires a specific type of foundational discipline to actively and consistently create worlds and visions that are *otherwise* to that which we have inherited from the dominant system of colonial thought.

Michel further offers a conceptualisation of 'the panopticon' in *Discipline and Punish*: this metaphor can also be read as a pertinent way to understand how such colonial disciplines operate in society today. The panopticon was an architectural idea initially designed by Enlightenment philosopher Jeremy Bentham to consider how to build efficiency and discipline within the prison. It was a watchtower in the centre of the prison that prisoners could not see into. This watchtower was surrounded by the prison cells wherein the prisoners did not know whether they were being watched or not. This was thought to produce circumstances in which prisoners behave as if they were being consistently watched, thus making this form of self-discipline a product of the real or imagined sense of surveillance. Michel Foucault (2020, p. 201) describes the intent of the panopticon as:

> to induce in the inmate a state of conscious and permanent visibility that assures the automatic functioning of power . . . the inmates should be caught up in a power situation of which they themselves are the bearers.

Put simply, one must self-discipline in this way by virtue of the fear of being caught. This therefore suggests there are other motivations within the prisoner, that is conceivably the desire to be free. It is almost taken for granted that the prisoner may want to 'misbehave' or escape the confines of the prison cell and therefore the external disciplinary force, real or imagined, is required to keep the prisoner incarcerated. I would, however, argue that it also requires another kind of discipline in and of itself to hold and maintain the flame of hope and a move towards strategies to free oneself in the context of the prison. To vehemently believe that one may escape from the prison cell, both the literal and the proverbial cells we may encounter in life, is a discipline of hope. That is to say that it requires a discreet, yet uncompromising, form of discipline that comes from the internal self to remain *Undisciplined* and not to succumb to the fullness of docility prescribed by external narrators of disciplinarity. To be an Undisciplined Scholar is a discipline arising from the self against a backdrop of colonial technologies of power that want us to acquiesce to docile approaches to the creation of knowledge, approaches that do not challenge the presiding colonial epistemological consensus. To be *Undisciplined* is to remain steadfast in the maintenance of hope and belief, even if our material conditions give no indication that freedom is possible.

On the Coloniality of Knowledge

Formations of Knowledge

The phrase 'Sapere Aude!' has been affectionately described and remembered as the rallying call of the European Enlightenment after Immanuel Kant expressed the powerful maxim in his essay 'What is Enlightenment?' This Latin phrase loosely translates to 'dare to know' or 'have the courage to use your own reason'. The Age of Enlightenment, or the Age of Science or Reason, was a crucial turning point in history in which the intellectual revolution transformed the European relationship to knowledge and truth, and through colonial force, that of the world. However, there is something quite ironic about Immanuel's invocation that one should dare to know, or use one's own reason – another translation being one should think for one's self – in that the Enlightenment offered a framework which policed firstly *who* could know, and secondly *how* one may come to know. So, whilst there may be some harsh critics of *Undisciplined* on many fronts such as the proposition that the abolition of the University is something that deserves serious intellectual and practical discussion, ironically in the spirit of *Sapere Aude* I am daring to think for myself. I am becoming undisciplined in my analysis of knowledge itself.

It is important to firstly understand more precisely the broad Enlightenment consensus on *who* can know and *how* one can come to know to understand the limitations Immanuel's *Sapere Aude* discreetly holds behind its veneer of beauty and simplicity. The Enlightenment saw the birth of the modern subject, that subject as body and mind, and is defined through the faculty of being a thinking, or reasoning, thing. This was established through Rene Descartes' famous Cogito – I think;

therefore, I am – or cogito ergo sum. Rene was making a meta-physical argument here concerning his own, and by extension other human's, foundational existence – that is how can we know that we exist, how can we know that we are human? For Rene that was through the knowledge that we possess the faculty of thought. Rene's impact on how we consider modern subjectivity has not been historically understated. 'I think, therefore I am', was articulated by Rene Descartes at the latter end of the Renaissance period and it became the refrain of the Enlightenment sung into the work of the Enlightenment's 'greatest' thinkers, and many of our contemporary intellectual leaders. Thus, the question of *who* can think is one of primary importance because the Cogito prescribes that who can think is who is human, and who is human is who can think – the construction of biological races greatly impacted the designation of humanity and who was then a *subject* and who was an *object*.

The idea of biological races, and its co-conspirator – racism, was a production of the epistemological project of the European Enlightenment; racial eugenics were proposed and accepted as a hard science in the positivist tradition, the tradition that holds that everything that is justifiable can be known through empirical evidence (Bashford and Levine, 2010). This is coa-lesced in the philosophical work of the time with Immanuel Kant's words in *Observations on the Feeling of the Beautiful and Sublime* that reflected his own beliefs, and those of David Hume – another of the most influential philosophers of the period – about the humanity, or lack thereof, of people who were not white:

> The Negroes of Africa have by nature no feeling that rises above the trifling. Mr Hume challenges anyone to cite a single exam-ple in which a Negro has shown talents . . . not a single one was ever found who presented anything great in art or science or any other praiseworthy quality. (Kant, 2011, p. 58)

This was written after pages of asserting the numerous qualities of white European people and thus juxtaposing Black Africans as their antithesis. What Immanuel has achieved here is to take Rene's assumption that to be human is to be a thinking thing, and to demonstrate through his 'scientific' and 'empirically' based observations that he could objectively ascertain that Black people do not hold the faculty of rationalist thought – and subsequently do not fall into the category of human. Thus, they cannot be subject, and are instead produced as object. This in turn devalues their indigenous epistemological frameworks and ways of being that may have not reflected the European way of knowing but were valid and important in their own right.

The work of theorists such as Frantz Fanon (2001, 2008) and Edward Said (2003) was instrumental in offering an understanding of the colonial subject, or object. Edward Said's critical theory, developed in a book of the same name, *Orientalism*, is where he demonstrates how the Orient (the East) was produced in contrast to the superior Occident (the West). Edward explores the ways in which the West consolidated its identity by creating a hierarchy in which it sat at the top as superior to all other geographies and races. Frantz Fanon (2008) also expresses that 'decolonization is truly the creation of new men. But such a creation cannot be attributed to a supernatural power: The "thing" colonized becomes a man through the very process of liberation' (p. 2). That is to say that colonial systems produced non-whites as less than human subjects – and therefore the process of decolonisation is not just about changes to the external world – it is also about the transformation of who then has access to the category of human. Therefore, if decolonisation is still a process that we are in, then we – non-white people – are still in the process of becoming human.

This intersection demonstrates the relationship between metaphysics and epistemology – we must establish *what* exists in order to know what knowledge is being created and validated because knowledge does not emerge from a vacuum – it emerges from what we consider to be reality. Thus, the continued colonial notion that people of colour are less than human, and therefore cannot produce knowledge, has a considerable impact on how racism is explicitly and implicitly constructed and negotiated throughout the world. What can be seen as a 'micro-aggression', such as a Black person being spoken over in a lecture theatre when offering their insight, or having their views disregarded in a meeting or on a TV set, is not an incident that can be considered in isolation. This is a reflection of the colonial notion that Black people lack the faculty of thought; and therefore, our views, insights, and knowledges can be so systematically and seamlessly overlooked. This is what critical Black feminist thinker and philosopher Patricia Hill Collins (2003) defines as the Eurocentric Masculinist Knowledge Validation Process, which I will continue to discuss the nature of in the chapters that follow.

The epistemological consensus that emerged through the Enlightenment period, and which now dominates the modern world, is the scientific method. 'Science' was used during this period to offer a proof for a biological basis of races and therefore legitimise the different treatment of races, hence racism. Science has gained such power and legitimacy in the world because it is considered inquiry that is entirely objective, and therefore can be trusted. I argue that nothing can be entirely objective and instead each researcher has biases and personal interests that are brought to the inquiry. For instance, the priorities of scientific development in the modern world are not simply isolated aims; they rest on human need and human ingenuity – as well as other factors such as wealth, location, and quite simply interest. Whilst scientific experiments can be largely controlled for results that maintain consistency, the road to coming to the experiment itself occurred in a social context with beliefs, bias, and changing ethical principles that impact the method and design of the experiment. Hence, I argue that objectivity is a fallacy.

Still, the issue here is not that the scientific method exists or that it demonstrates bias and inconsistencies; it is instead that this method exists on the premise that it is the only valid route to create and validate knowledge in the world. When we consider the passage of colonisation, we often think of the land that was captured and colonised, the people that were harmed in the process, and the resources that were pillaged though this focus in and of itself reflects the dominance of the scientific method. A method that is focused on understanding phenomena exclusively on the basis on what can be observed through a five-sensory experience, a materialist lens, and thus proven by modern science. The *epistemological* violence that took place through the passage of European colonisation can broadly be historicised as beginning in 1492 with Columbus's landing in the Americas, and it is important to recognise that it is still in flow. This was a process that was indeed about the capture of land, people, and resources, but it was also the process of suppressing and invalidating all other routes to the creation and validation of knowledge. This harmful process was a systematic dispossession of the colonial subject/object, which invoked a belief that not only could the subaltern not speak, as argued in Spivak's (2004) seminal essay 'Can the subaltern speak?', but that the subaltern could not think. This has been aptly defined by Boaventura de Sousa Santos (2007) as *epistemicide* – the extermination of ways of knowing and knowledge systems that did not adhere to the Eurocentric model of knowing.

Epistemicide

Ramon Grosfoguel (2013) argues in his decisive paper 'The structure of knowledge in Westernized universities: epistemic racism/sexism and the four genocides/epistemicides of the long 16th century', that men of five countries (Italy, France,

England, Germany, and the United States) have defined the canon of knowledge that dominates the modern world. He defines this as epistemic privilege and compares it to the epistemic inferiority of all knowledges that did not emanate from European men of these nations, thus highlighting the racism and sexism that mediate epistemic relations. This clearly and succinctly outlines the process of epistemicide in that the European project positioned itself superior to any knowledge or system they had 'discovered' or were yet to discover. This means that prior to any connection or knowledge of a different system, the European man approached it with the belief that he was superior, that he held the truth to teach (read: dominate) the lesser other.

Ramon builds on the work of fellow Latin American decolonial theorist Enrique Dussel, who has offered a great contribution to our collective understanding of the impact of Eurocentric philosophy and the critical requirement of decoloniality as a way to move beyond modernity, a move he labels transmodernity (Grosfoguel, 2013). In the essay Ramon particularly works with Enrique's critique of Cartesian philosophy offering the argument of 'I conquer, therefore I am', which he argues preceded the Cartesian Cogito by 150 years, and Ramon extends this into 'I exterminate, therefore I am'. Ramon is concerned with understanding the ways that we may be able to track the relationship between genocides carried out by European and Northern American colonial powers, and how these were concurrently epistemicides with the impact of suppressing and in the end exterminating knowledge systems. The presupposition of I conquer, or I exterminate as opposed to the Cartesian I think, offers us a different way to consider the European and Eurocentric *I am*. That is to say that to be human, to be validated in one's existence, one must conquer or exterminate, and without this impetus one is not human – one does not exist. So, existence has been something that is defined in opposition to an either real or imagined other (read: threat) that must be dominated to affirm one's existence. This is the approach that narrated colonial epistemicide. The coloniality of knowledge did not only favour the scientific method above other forms of knowledge creation and validation – it created a framework in which other forms of knowledge *had* to be eradicated. The approach of needing to annihilate or conquer the 'other' when brought into contact demonstrates a level of persistent fear towards anything or anyone that is different or outside of their epistemic purview. It is quite an irony when considering what is being purported is a knowledge system that claims to hold objectivity as being of prime importance but it is arguably the feeling, the emotional and embodied experience, of fear that drives the fierce protection of the Eurocentric model of knowledge – this is a critical reflection I was able to marry words to when in conversation with the brilliant scholar, artist, and pleasure activist Ama Josephine Budge.

4

A Note to the Self

I would like you to pause in the process of reading this book. Pause, and breathe.

Breathe deeply through your nose until your body is filled with gentle air, hold on to it for a few moments.

Release it through your mouth.

Repeat this a few times.

How do you feel?

How does your body feel?

I offer this experience, this creation of space through the breath, almost to expand and extend time. The breath is undeniably powerful. It is with us from the moment we are born to the last moment we lay to rest. The great mystics and spiritual teachers of the world have taught us how important and transformative the breath is, how important that pause is.

The Buddhist teachings remind us of mindfulness as a pillar of the eight-fold path, Patanjali's yoga sutras offer us

Pranayama – the breath – as one of the eight limbs of yoga (al-Bīrūnī, Kozah, and White, 2022), Christian theology remarks *be still and know that I am God.* That stillness is when we are able to recognise the presence of divinity. The sciences teach us that the breath supports us in the transition from the sympathetic nervous system to the parasympathetic nervous system, which results in a peaceful and relaxed state being achieved within the body.

When I positioned the premise of this book in its early stages to colleagues, friends, and comrades, the response was often one of shock or disapproval. It was interesting to witness, both visibly and also on an energetic level, the fear-based and closed responses to the possibility of such a work.

To abolish the university? The premise abhorred so many. So, I shifted and told people that it is simply a thought experiment. I saw people settle and become more open to this proposition. It was as if provided nothing *actually* happens to our sacred institutions of higher learning, and this is just an intellectual and theoretical experiment, it can be explored. For me, this was quite the indictment on the utility of theory, that whether consciously or unconsciously many academics saw theory as distinct from practice. That there is no danger that theory may actually become practice, so it is a safe playground for the whimsical.

It made me think about how so many of us have invested our identities within the institution.

Who are you without the university?

Who am I without the university?

It felt that I was attacking their sense of self, their space of safety and meaning. Whenever we project our sense of self into anything outside of ourselves, then the loss of, or threat to, that thing will be experienced as a lack of safety and a threat to our survival. Many of us are invested in the institution for various reasons, meaning that its demise could offer a legitimate threat to our physical survival, and a more unconscious threat to the survival of our ego or sense of self. For academics, the university pays our wages, the university has offered us a space to do the intellectual work we love, the university has offered us prestige and something to be proud of, the university has offered us both intellectual and social community. It is of course understandable why many would not immediately support a rejection of the institution in its entirety. Though the work of abolition is not to simply destroy, it is to rebuild. It is to create the space within our imaginations that may allow us to dream up visions of a world in which all our physical and emotional needs are met beyond the structures of harmful institutions. It is to create different possibilities for ourselves and to recognise that all of that which we love can take place beyond the institution.

I am further concerned we have built this false image that the university is a place of virtuosity. We are able to sit in our Ivory Towers and critique the entire expanse of society and the natural world and not once question the role of the university in the world. It is almost as if we critique the rest of the world enough, we place ourselves as the commentators, or more concerningly the referees, of the social and natural world, offering academics both a place of immunity and somewhat superiority.

In the summer of 2022, I attended the League of European Research Universities Summer School as part of my doctoral studies, held at the University of Utrecht in The Netherlands. The theme was *The University of the Future*, exploring what needs to change within the institution to create a better future for the university. I of course contested whether the university has a future at all. The conference lasted a week, and at the start I was almost heckled down by other students for offering such a viewpoint that most of them fiercely disagreed with. By the end of the week after deep and stretching conversations, the building of connection and community, as well as the limits and the harms of the institution demonstrating itself in various ways, many were coming around to the idea. On the final day of the conference, I walked out of the concluding session as one of the heads of a European higher education organisation aggressively spoke over a woman of colour and told her that her experiences and points of view were essentially worthless. This was not the first time I had witnessed such behaviour, often finding myself on the brutal end of it. I said all that I had to say in front of the room and left the space. I decided to make the most of my final hours in The Netherlands and smoked a joint I had purchased at a coffee shop in Amsterdam earlier that week. I sat and allowed time to stretch and bend as I took a pause and sat in the square opposite University Hall, Utrecht, and witnessed my mind alter in state. Soon the other students and academics surrounded me, and many offered their recognition that the points I had made earlier in the week about university abolition were indeed beginning to make sense. Their defences had fallen, and their hearts were open to the possibility that the transformation that needs to take place when considering the future of the university is to consider whether it is to have a future at all. Their minds, too, had been altered.

So, this interval between the pages of this text offers a space to take a moment with the self to explore what may be coming up for you. A capitalist and scientific culture teaches us that the more that we continue to actively *do* and work, the further we get in terms of development and breakthroughs. The great mystics over the centuries have taught us that in the pause, in the silence, in the break, is when we find the greatest leaps forward.

That is to extend and expand time as we know it, when we are able to pause, to go inwardly and explore what parts of ourselves may be in gravest resistance to different and novel ideas. To sit with the scared and fearful parts of ourselves, to feel so secure within ourselves that we might be able to renegotiate our identities and evolve our sense of self in the face of different information. That when we slow down and pause, the strides we are able to make in knowledge and within the self are vast. That is how we bend and shape and alter the passage of time. That is how we create new worlds; it begins with creating the space to allow the possibility into our hearts and realities.

Let us continue this journey.

5

A Spiritual Intervention

In the opening to *The Creative Act: A Way of Being*, Rick Rubin – a music producer and mogul who co-founded Def Jam Records – begins by letting us as the reader know that 'nothing in this book is known to be true . . . [some ideas] may awaken an inner knowing you forgot you had' (Rubin, 2023). In this opening Rick is speaking to this unmanifest reality, this 'inner knowing', this deeper look into oneself as the heart of creative work, of creative living. Rick has worked with an illustrious list of some of the most successful music artists in the world and he speaks of his work as essentially looking for a 'feeling', to understand how a piece of music makes him feel, and relaying that back to the artist is his primary way of working (*Rick Rubin: The 60 Minutes Interview*, 2023).

Equally, Julia Cameron (2016) makes a similar argument in her bestselling work *The Artist's Way* wherein she offers readers a 12-week course aimed at recovering their creative selves. In this manual Julia explores how we might navigate accessing this higher part of ourselves, of our consciousness, which she refers to as a spiritual journey.

So, what does this have to do with decoloniality?

The creative arts are quite possibly one of the most beautiful directions we can cast our eyes to find what a praxis of decolonial work may look like. The two writers I have mentioned above are racialised as white; however, they speak to what I consider the heart of work that revokes a colonial framing. In this chapter I explore how colonial work was, and is, tied up with an exorcism of spirit and spirituality from daily life. Epistemicide was at the heart of the colonial mission and here I argue that the knowledge that was eradicated was spiritual knowledge. That is spiritual knowledge not in a religious sense, but in a recognition that knowledge exists within us all, within the self, and it does not always need to be witnessed, ratified, and validated by a scholarly community to be verified as *true*.

This is the knowledge of self, and knowledge that descends from realms that are imperceptible to the rationalist scientific mode of knowledge production and validation – the 'inner knowing' that Rick invokes above. For me, considering alternative ways of knowing and coming to know should be the heart and the essence of the project of decolonisation – for two key reasons: (1) prior to colonisation, across formerly colonised peoples, alternative ways of knowing were the foundation of being and becoming, and (2) because when we open up the possibility of alternative ways of knowing and deciding upon truth and action, we open up possibilities for other ways of thinking, existing, and (re)making the world.

Genealogy, Witches, and Decolonisation

Here I will rethink the history of coloniality through the method of genealogy. Genealogy, as offered by Michel Foucault, is a method of writing critical histories that explore what role knowledge and power play in creating our collective present. In his article exploring Michel's development of this concept, David Garland (2014) writes:

Genealogical analysis traces how contemporary practices and institutions emerged out of specific struggles, conflicts, alliances, and exercises of power, many of which are nowadays forgotten. It thereby enables the genealogist to suggest – not by means of normative argument but instead by presenting a series of troublesome associations and lineages – that institutions and practices we value and take for granted today are actually more problematic or more 'dangerous' than they otherwise appear. The point of genealogy is not to search for 'origins' . . . It is, rather, as its name suggests, a search for processes of *descent* and of *emergence* . . . Its point is not to think historically about the past but rather to use historical materials to rethink the present.

This offers a way to think through what I argue is a critical foundation of colonial expansion that is not always considered as related to the emergence of colonial missions. Reconsidering, or expanding, our thinking about the roots/routes through which coloniality came into being, and of our current relationship to the afterlives (and in some cases present lives) of colonial expansion, offers us more complexity, and further tools to employ in thinking through how we might address, more effectively, coloniality in our modern world.

Spirituality in its various forms dominated the pre-modern world. Across the former colonies, polytheistic spirituality was a primary route to knowledge and truth. This was also true in Europe with pagan traditions such as Wicca and Gnosticism being prevalent until the suppression by the Church. I'd argue it was the mission of the Church to first suppress this across Europe, which was demonstrated through the extensive witch hunts and subsequent witch trials and executions, and then to continue this suppression in the colonies under the guise of 'saving' them. It is estimated that between 40,000 and 60,000 people, majority women, were executed across Europe on account of charges related to witchcraft during the sixteenth, seventeenth, and eighteenth centuries (Burton Russell, 2023). Similarly, in the newly colonised North America, witches were harshly pursued: the infamous Salem witch trials of 1692–3 articulated the mass hysteria stirred up in the people to create witches as the enemy and a threat to all. The word 'witch' is still often used as a harsh insult to describe a woman that has engaged in activities that are perceived as evil or mean-spirited, demonstrating the ongoing gendered demonisation of polytheistic spirituality. The experience of witches in Europe during this time demonstrates a specific form of epistemic violence towards the *other* within the European population.

So, what I want us to think through as a direct precursor to colonial missions is the suppression of indigenous spirituality within Western Europe, and by this, I mean spiritualities that were prominent across peoples indigenous to the Celtic, Hellenistic, Germanic, and Basque regions. This is different from arguments concerning the extension and imposition of the Church into previously colonised lands. The difference is subtle yet important, as the Church and its missionaries played a key role in colonial expansion, as has been well documented. However, as Silvia Federici (2021) argues, African enslavement and the witch hunts can be understood as two sides of the same coin. Silvia prescribes this relationship specifically to capitalism, and equally Ramon Grosfoguel touches on this in his essay 'The structure of knowledge in Westernized universities: epistemic racism/sexism and the four genocides/epistemicides of the long 16th century', where he comments that very few people have made this linkage other than Silvia Federici, though he notes her work is focused on political economy as opposed to epistemology. With this genocide/epistemicide, Ramon offers the pertinent recognition that in this case there were no books to burn as knowledge was passed down through generations; the Indo-European women's bodies were the 'books' and so were incinerated at the stake. Ramon links this genocide/epistemicide of Indo-European women and the indigenous knowledges they held to the exportation of Christian theology and to patriarchy, both points I would echo in importance. However, what I argue is missing here is the more explicit linkage of this relationship between the genocides of Indo-European women and European colonial expansion, which I have argued was a direct precursor. Equally, deeper analysis of the nature of the knowledge itself that these women held is omitted – this genocide/epistemicide was also the rooting out of an empowered way of knowing, a way of knowing that requires no intercessors other than one's own personal connection to their divinity and land. To colonise a people, you must teach them that their ways of knowing are insufficient, you must make them reliant on a power outside of themselves and their traditional ways of coming to know. I argue that this is core to the suppression and genocidal violence against the witches of Europe, and this was mirrored in colonial violence against people of formally colonised lands, who had ways of knowing that drew from a spiritual source known to reside in each and every person – colonial violence severed them from their own divine source.

As a person of Ghanaian descent, born and raised in Europe due to the afterlives of colonisation, on my journey of decolonial discovery and spiritual expansion I have developed my own spiritual practice which creolises different forms of spirituality from across the world. A core part of that practice is the reading of tarot cards, which descends from the Hellenistic period in ancient Italy. Alongside this, I draw from ancient Akan and broader Sub-Saharan African traditions of ancestor veneration. Similarly, I am an avid student of astrology and regularly read my own and others' birth charts using the Hellenistic system, and I am equally a student of yoga and Vedic traditions. What I have come to believe about spirituality is that it is not necessarily about the method of divination, or the name of the deities in different traditions – instead it is a journey that asks one to return to themselves. To acknowledge and revere the divinity that lays within themselves, this has led me to think of different approaches to spirituality from around the world almost like different languages. Each has its own unique way of communicating, and perhaps there are idiosyncratic accents that define a particular way of engaging a spiritual tradition, though all lead to a presence of divine energy in every single sentient being, and within the land that holds us.

Decoloniality Is a Spiritual Matter

When we consider the cause and intentions of colonial projects, in the academy we often point to causes such as the, at the time, newly produced racial 'sciences', and economic and geopolitical incentives as the key drivers of colonisation. However, as I have argued, the witch trials and the suppression of polytheistic nature-based forms of spirituality across the Western world at the presage of the Enlightenment period equally foreshadowed the colonisation of lands. The suppression of these traditions was not just a by-product of the imposition of Christian theology; there was something specific within these traditions that had to be rooted out if colonial expansion was to endure.

So, when the Western man came into contact with the Other through the passage of colonisation, I argue he was not abhorred by race alone, but was driven to dominate and destroy on the basis of the now formally colonised holding belief systems that were reflective of those beliefs the Western man killed within himself – and so must therefore exterminate within the other. They must kill without what is most detestable within.

Much of what we consider decolonial thought is important; however, it is insufficient in resolving the question of coloniality as the question extends beyond race, culture, geopolitics, and economics. It is equally a question of material and immaterial. It is such a wonder how so much decolonial thought and theory can entirely miss the discussion of spirituality and occultist practices. It often offers the content of alternative knowledges as a discursive matter, that is to say that it is more important to understand that alternative knowledges exist than it is to meaningfully engage with these knowledges. This is theories such as the pluriverse (Reiter, 2018; de Sousa Santos and Martins, 2021), which argues that we must exist within a pluriverse of knowledge as the remedy for coloniality. However, this theory does not meaningfully engage with what is required of both science and other knowledges, such as spiritual knowledges, to be able to exist concurrently – my belief is that science would have to transform in meaning and be accepted as not the whole of truth but merely a discourse of truth – but this in itself changes the definition of scientific fact. Nor does it consider the work that must be done on the collective psyche so that it does not simply reinvoke the form of epistemicide discussed as alternative knowledges gain prominence. *Undisciplined* both in form and content is an attempt to meaningfully engage with phenomena beyond that which is considered acceptable or even provable within the Western tradition, to move us closer to a decolonial (read: spiritual) analysis of the world.

Spirituality is decoloniality; decoloniality is spirituality.

I speak in such definite terms about spiritual knowledge as *the* alternative knowledge – not to invoke binary understandings of knowledge but instead as a representation of the world pre-colonial (read: spiritual) and postcolonial (read: scientific). With this, spiritual in and of itself infers multiple and quite possibly **infinite** ways of coming to know, so whilst on the face of it this may seem to be a binary, when we hold the notion of the 'spiritual' in its truest ever-unfurling form, we understand that this is not a binary at all.

Epistemicide Continued

Steve Biko (1987, p. 93), in 'Black consciousness and the quest for true humanity', demonstrates this relationship between coloniality and the colonisation of polytheistic spiritual belief systems. He explores how monotheistic Christianity was deemed by the coloniser as being the religion of science and other spiritual belief systems as mere superstition that must be rooted out:

> The first people to come and relate to blacks in a human way in South Africa were the missionaries. They were in the vanguard of the colonisation movement to 'civilise and educate' the savages and introduce the Christian message to them. The religion they brought was quite foreign to the black indigenous people ... It was the missionaries who confused the people with their new religion. They scared our people with stories of hell. They painted their God as a demanding God who wanted worship 'or else'. People had to discard their clothes and their customs in order to be accepted in this new religion. Knowing how religious the African people were, the missionaries stepped up their terror campaign on the emotions of the people with their detailed accounts of eternal burning, tearing of hair and gnashing of teeth. By some strange and twisted logic, they argued that theirs was a scientific religion and ours a superstition.

Steve recognises the missionaries as the vanguard of the colonial movement: that to capture the spirit of the African people was what laid down the framework for the rest of the colonial mission to ensue, and ultimately succeed. A similar sentiment is offered in Malidoma Patrice Somé's (1995) narrative autobiography *Of Water and Spirit* wherein he tells the story of the *literal*, not proverbial, magical ways of the precolonial tribe he heralded from. He recalls memories where he details how a room he was in turned over on itself and was upside down after his grandfather invoked the spirits. Malidoma was from the Dagara tribe of Burkina Faso and his story is one in which at a young age he was kidnapped by French missionaries and raised in a Catholic convent to be taught out of the ways of his people. In *Of Water and Spirit* the retelling of the reality of Patrice's life in many parts brings into sharp contention our scientific understanding of reality, for instance the example I have offered above does not cohere with the laws of gravity.

In this way, the critique I have levelled against the conceptualisation of the pluriverse does not hold in that if we are to take science as it has been narrated – i.e., unchangeable truth – then alternative knowledges that conflict with scientific laws cannot be held in the pluriverse unless we challenge the nature of science itself. This challenge would argue that at times scientific 'fact' is fallible in the face of alternative metaphysical eventualities under certain conditions.

A Note on Shame

I attended a talk in Berlin whilst on a trip to Germany in the winter of 2022 – the discussion was about health and wellness with a specific focus on the speaker's experiences with psychedelic medicines. After the discussion I went to speak to him more once the crowd had begun to trickle out of the event space. I informed him of some of my research interests concerning alternative ways to produce and validate knowledge, specifically ways that do not necessarily adhere to the scientific method. The conversation led the speaker to open up about various experiences he had after taking psychedelic medicines; he admitted he felt he had traversed different dimensions and witnessed the unthinkable, but felt he could not share these experiences on stage because he feared everyone would think he was 'crazy'. This confession helped me to understand that the knowledge system is also mediated by shame, and not necessarily just by scientific truth in the way we are taught to believe it is. Shame erupts within us when we experience or believe things that are not commonly held as true within either scientific fact or societal norms of monotheistic religions. In the writing of this work, shame is a blockade I am consistently working at navigating through to speak my truth with honesty and openness knowing the less than positive view of such spiritual practices within the academy.

Hence, to engage in undisciplined scholarly commitment is to navigate shame in the pursuit of a commitment to honesty and openness. The formations of knowledge are not just about what is true and what is untrue – it is also about what we can bear to be criticised about. That is to say: I believe in my work so much that I am willing for it to be torn apart and any negative connotations be extended to me as a person.

Scholarly work is, and should be, vulnerable work.

Further, through the passage of history we have seen what has happened to those that do not hold science as the single truth of the world – many have been burned at the stake, others have been suppressed, colonised, and enslaved. History has taught us, both consciously and subconsciously, this shame of claiming truth outside of the scientific method as a mode of self-protection. To not believe the scientific method was representative of the whole, at times meaning literal death. As mentioned, it requires a profound discipline to remain *undisciplined* in a world that shames alternative ways of viewing the world, and of viewing knowledge, though it is our right and duty to think for ourselves – *Sapre Aude* – even against a backdrop unable to validate our beliefs, or one that is accomplished in shaming us into submission of the epistemological consensus of Enlightenment thought.

6

Knowledge, Discipline(s), and the University

The University and Its Disciplines

I have loved the university. There are few things in life that satisfy me more than the pursuit of knowledge; the desire for me to learn something new each day comes as readily as that to nourish my body with food. When I am not in the pursuit of knowledge, I find myself sad, restless, and disconnected. To some this may seem hyperbolic – but I believe all lives have a core purpose – and I am grateful to have found mine, which is in the beauty of the endless exploration of knowledge and belief. Perhaps a way to understand this is that knowledge gives me the dopamine fix my neurodivergent mind seeks, but a truer explanation for me is that the philosophical search for knowledge and 'truth' connects with the deepest part of me – it feels like the work of my soul. Hence, the university seemed like the most obvious home. At a point I did consider committing my life to academia – finding a tenured role at a prestigious school in the States and working my way up to a role which allowed me to impact student education across the institution. When you are so profoundly in love with something, as I am with the pursuit of knowledge, it comes so naturally to want to share that love and passion with others and I saw this potential within the university.

On this account I was protective of the institution, I believed in her ability to change and transform – to decolonise her hardened walls. I saw such beauty in her curvatures, felt peace in her hallowed halls, and the idea I would ever consider her demise was unthinkable. However, my pursuit of knowledge has led me to what feels like the borders and boundaries of the institution. If I am to continue to honour the truth of where this pursuit has guided me, the university can no longer be my home, nor can I be quiet about her unyielding commitment to colonial epistemes. As mentioned, my first discipline in the academy was philosophy. I was fascinated, and still very much am, by asking some of the most fundamental and foundational questions of life. I was attracted by what I had perceived to be its unendingness, to sit and reflect on questions that have no definite answers but value was found in the journey of the questioning itself. What I actually found when encountering philosophy, particularly at a European University, was a rigid form of analytical enquiry that did not allow for any of the questioning I had expected. As mentioned earlier in the text, I feel I had to build up a form of learnt forgetfulness in order to pass my philosophy degree. This is because the discipline required me to forget my own experiences of the world and phenomena in order to adhere to its rigid approach enough to get the degree I was paying for. It seemed the only questions I was able to ask to challenge the theories of the white men I was presented with were those already asked by other white men validated within the discipline. I had to forget the racial dimensions of ethical questions; in my final year Feminist Philosophy course I had to forget that intersectionality was a viable lens to explore gender through; I had to skip past the many pages of the texts I was required to purchase in an attempt to forget that the philosophers we were studying spent a considerable amount of time 'philosophising' about the intellectual and cultural inadequacies of Black people.

In 'On the theory of ideology – The politics of Althusser', Jacques Rancière (1974) explores exactly this and remarks that Philosophy as a discipline holds a specific irony in that it attempts to question knowledge without ever touching the foundations of the knowledge itself. He further argues that all inquiry within the subject of philosophy results in a restoration of the discipline. This is to say that if your philosophical work is not in accord with the fundamental beliefs held in the landscape of the discipline, it will not be considered as 'good' philosophy – regardless of its value. Boaventura de Sousa Santos (2007) further echoes this sentiment in his paper 'Beyond abyssal thinking: from global lines to ecologies of knowledges', wherein he argues that Western thought continues to exclude alternative philosophies through a focus on debating internal differences, as opposed to recognising that other philosophical traditions even exist.

Still, it is important to mention that this rigidity may not be true for schools of Philosophy across the world. The American Philosophical Society recognised Africana Philosophy as a developing field in the 1980s (Outlaw Jr. and Jeffers, 2022). Equally, we are seeing the growing exploration of Chinese philosophy throughout the Western academy. Roger T. Ames (2017) examined this in his paper 'Better late than never: understanding Chinese philosophy and "translating it" into the western academy'. In this paper Roger examined the challenges of translation beyond language, and explored how importing Chinese philosophy to a Judeo-Christian culture can require a compromising of its truth, specifically when concerning a connection to spirituality or religion. This is because of the limited conception of 'religion' in Western thought, as necessarily being related to a God. So, whilst alternative philosophies may be appearing in Philosophy departments and in philosophical research, arguably the disciplines within the

Western academy cannot facilitate the complexity and truth of these philosophical traditions because they are so deeply tied up with spirituality. How one connects to spirituality and facilitates a spiritual connection is beyond the methodological standard of the Western academic tradition, which is often limited to studying only those who observe spirituality from an anthropological or ethnographic viewpoint – as opposed to an embodied understanding of the spiritual self. Hence important, and even fundamental, intricacies of these traditions can be wholly lost through the process of academic research.

Further, I have often queried whether there has been an intentional guarding of the discipline of Philosophy. This can be seen in the knowledge that is encountered, and how one is *allowed* to encounter it, but also with who is in schools of Philosophy, which I would argue is an extension of the inherent colonial commitments that exist within the episte-mological hardlines of the discipline. It guards both in terms of knowledge and in terms of body/minds. A recent study took an inventory of all the Philosophy departments across the United Kingdom, over the years 2019–20, to understand trends in the teaching of subjects concerning the philosophy of race. They found that in 1,166 modules surveyed only one was a dedicated module to the Philosophy of Race – this is less than 0.1%. Further, of 728 Philosophy staff research website profiles investigated, just 23 noted an interest in the Philosophy of Race – this equates to around 3% (Chauhan *et al.*, 2022). This damn-ing study demonstrates the state of Philosophy in the British academy. Whilst I was unable to find recent figures in terms of the racial make-up of these Philosophy departments, in 2014 there were just five Black teaching or research staff working in any department of Philosophy across the entire UK, and none of them were Professors (Jahi, 2014). I am aware the landscape has somewhat changed since, markedly with the appointment of Professor Tommy J. Curry at the University of Edinburgh, a Black Professor of Philosophy, whose research interests speak to so much that has been silenced across the philosophical field in the UK such as the philosophical questions of Black manhood. Still, this and other isolated breakthroughs in departments of Philosophy across the UK have not gone far enough in challenging the biases this discipline demonstrates. I have often wondered about the roots of this guarding around the study of philosophy at the European University, and in the following I will do my best to explain what I believe could conceivably fuel it.

Philosophy forms the foundations of every other discipline in the Western academy; this is very pronounced across the arts, social sciences, and humanities, but this is also true across the hard sciences. In the Western tradition, the philosophers were the mediators of what constitutes reality: this of course is the study of metaphysics. Further, philosophers were also the mediators of knowledge itself – in that the question of what constitutes knowledge was a question reserved for the philosophical field of epistemology, and similarly the philosophical study of ethics necessarily permeates every discipline. Each discipline has a framework for what constitutes reality, valid knowledge, and for the ethical principles that dictate research. With this, I argue that Philosophy is the cornerstone of the Western academy. Scientists ask questions about the nature of our reality based on the philosophical consensus that our reality in some way exists. Further, all other disciplines also rely on this metaphysical assumption, but also on the epistemological framework of how knowledge and truth are found to form the foundation for their frameworks of inquiry. So, this is to say that if Philosophy were to become infiltrated – I use this language as infiltration is what would be required for such a discipline to change – the entirety of the Western academy is destabilised. The inflexibility and intentional unchangingness of this discipline are deeply political and upon which the survival and continuation of the Western academy relies.

The way I visualise the academy is that Philosophy is placed at the centre and all other disciplines are organised around its milieu. In my own studies I made what I would consider a strategic move into the discipline of Sociology from my master's studies onwards, so that I could ask the questions Philosophy would not allow or validate within its framework. Ironically many of these questions are philosophical – however, I could not see, at that time, a school of Philosophy welcoming my approach and it meeting their academic standards. Arguably Sociology is seen as a less respected discipline – I have had people laugh when I say I am doing a doctorate in Sociology and even attribute it to the only reason I would have been admitted to Cambridge; that is to suggest if I were to study something 'real' or 'respectable', I would not be at the university. Withstanding the blatant racism and classism inherent in these comments – it also demonstrates the way Sociology is viewed with little legitimacy by some. However, I often call Sociology the discipline that moves. Coming from Philosophy, Sociology felt limber in its approach to study: there was more openness to different methodologies and the ability to question far more. Most importantly, it allowed me to begin exploring some of the philosophical questions that had most occupied my mind and spirit through the study of 'social theory' such as Critical Race Theory, Black feminisms, and alternative epistemic approaches. I believe some of these questions are able to be explored because Sociology is not the foundation of the academy. Another way to think of it is as an arborescent structure: Sociology would perhaps be a fruit that the tree grew to bear as opposed to its very core roots and steadfast structure that Philosophy represents – if you are to look upon the fruit and alter it in some way, this does not change the structure or the nature of the tree. However, if you were to pull out its roots or slice through its bark, the entire tree dies – to me, this is what Philosophy represents for the Western university. Still, the further I go into study and the more I challenge the Eurocentric model of knowledge, the harder asking these questions in Sociology is becoming. There is still a core respectability to the study of Philosophy that I believe each discipline to some extent is committed to maintaining, as to deviate too far is to plunge the discipline itself into contention and face questions of its own validity. That discipline would face being stricken from the tree. With this we are able to understand the disciplining nature of disciplines. Each discipline has its rules and frameworks and methods and systems. When one spills beyond these strict parameters, discipline through words, questions, grading systems, and at times shaming is engaged to bring the researcher or student back in line. To discipline is to produce docile students and researchers that care more about adhering to the discipline, as this is what is required to pass, than they do about the integrity of study and true exploration.

In recent years the push towards interdisciplinary study has dominated discussions across higher education. This has been seen as a great innovation to improve student education and encourage a more holistic approach. For example, the London Interdisciplinary School opened its doors in 2017 and is the first institution to be granted full degree-awarding powers in the UK since 1960 (BBC News, 2020a), demonstrable of this turn to interdisciplinarity. However, there is a great difference between being interdisciplinary and being undisciplined. To work with multiple disciplines, which I would argue is better than the single disciplinary approach, is still rooted in harmful disciplining boundaries that curb the ability of radical thought and radical imagination.

One approach that attempts to remedy this has been to decolonise specific subject disciplines. The works of Ali Meghji (2021), Robbie Shilliam (2021), and Julian Go (2013, 2017) offer this decolonial approach to the discipline in the realms of Sociology and Politics. These are theorists whose work I deeply respect. I am blessed to be supervised by Ali Meghji at Cambridge and learn so much each time we meet. However,

intellectually we diverge as I believe the approach of decolonising a discipline is both a fallacy and a contradiction in terms
and meaning. The hopeful offerings that we might be able to
decolonise the disciplines do begin with an acknowledgement
the disciplines have been structured in the context of colonial
violence, but there is a redemptive essence present in these
theories. Broadly the arguments are similar to the pluriversal
arguments (Reiter, 2018; de Sousa Santos and Martins, 2021),
in that a recognition of indigenous epistemological traditions
is argued for and the idea that horizontal, as opposed to hier-
archical, conversations can be had between the Eurocentric
tradition alongside alternative ways of knowing, as inherent
to the rehabilitation of the disciplines. However, there is often
an engagement with the discursive need for indigenous epistemologies but scarcely is there a meaningful engagement with
what these would constitute. Indigenous epistemologies at
times will not meet the Eurocentric masculinist knowledge-
validation process and therefore struggle to gain any form of
horizontal legitimacy within the academy in the spaces where
contradiction with the presiding knowledge-validation process
is present. The example above from Roger Ames (2017), of
how Chinese Philosophy becomes disciplined in its true relation to spirituality when placed within the Western academy,
is demonstrative of this. Given the history of coloniality and
epistemicide, I struggle to see an eventuality in which the
'I conquer' does not re-invoke itself in the arena of knowledge.
What we would instead witness is indigenous knowledges
becoming disciplined in an inauthentic way within the academy in an effort to adhere to the structures and boundaries of
the knowledge validation process. We cannot decolonise the
discipline; disciplinarity is inherently colonial.

The Panopticon of Knowledge

A pioneer of Critical Race Theory and key philosopher of race, Charles W. Mills (2022) wrote the seminal text *The Racial Contract*, which critically explores the essential role race has played in shaping the political philosophy of the Western world. He opens the text by remarking that 'white supremacy is the unnamed political system that has made the modern world what it is today' (p. 1). I would argue that white supremacy and Eurocentrism can be used interchangeably here. He goes on to say, 'the system of domination by which white people have historically ruled over . . . is not seen as a political system at all' (pp. 1–2). Here, Charles is addressing the sinister nature of universality in white supremacy and Eurocentrism – its ability to define itself as nothing at all; simply, as the universal norm. Maldonado-Torres (2004), a leading decolonial theorist, consolidates this in his paper 'The topology of being and the geopolitics of knowledge', in which he describes the trend of European thinkers to erase the truths of colonialization and race, and when writing about the West and modernity, he describes this as 'the forgetfulness of coloniality' (p. 30), as a 'will-to-ignorance . . . the forgetfulness of damnation . . . a state of amnesia that leads to murder and destruction and epistemic will to power' (p. 36). This demonstrates the strategy of Eurocentric epistemology to occupy the centre of knowledge whilst at the same time constructing a discourse claiming that there is nothing at the centre at all. This is why much of what is actually a Eurocentric approach to creating and validating knowledge has come to be understood or labelled as 'common sense'; with this comes routine shaming for anyone that does not adhere to this form of 'common sense'. For example, to believe that a scientific understanding of the world is representative of the whole and nothing exists beyond this is often considered common sense and to propose otherwise is seen as ludicrous. To be placed at the centre whilst claiming there is nothing at the centre at all is also a way that Eurocentrism is able to beset any contestation against it as unnecessary at best, dangerous at worst. If nothing is at the centre, there is nothing to contest. As mentioned earlier, Grosfoguel (2013) explores the fact that the canon in the disciplines of the Social Sciences and Humanities is based on the thought of a few men from five Western countries and this is considered the norm and justified. The system works in a way such that if anyone is to challenge this strange and limited worldview, they are the one that is seen as a radical, as a problem.

For these reasons, I consider Eurocentric thought to form a panoptical dominance over knowledge. Just as the invisible guard created self-governing and self-disciplining within the prisoners, so too does Eurocentric thought create this self-disciplining within the subjects of the university and beyond. The university facilitates a disconnection from the self through offering a framework that defines what is legitimate and what is illegitimate. If anyone is to behave or create knowledge that does not adhere to its dictates of what valid knowledge can be, or the process through which it can be created, the university has numerous ways to discipline its subjects. In Paulo Freire's (2017) critical work *Pedagogy of the Oppressed*, he explores this very occurrence where he expresses 'the oppressed, having internalised the image of the oppressor and adopted his guidelines, are fearful of freedom' (p. 21). Paulo suggests there are times in which the oppressor does not need to extend their control over the subject as the subject has already internalised the guidelines the oppressor set out. For me this is again a demonstration of the panoptical dominance an oppressive system can take on. Further, as Paulo argues that the oppressed can even become fearful of freedom, there may too be a part of us that is actually fearful of what that freedom entails. We can become so accustomed and familiarised with an oppressive system that freedom from it actually appears as danger – and this is the place I feel many of us have come to with coloniality and the university.

To read the Foucauldian Panopticon with the Jungian unconscious brings us even closer to understanding how the panopticon of knowledge operates within us all. According to Carl Jung, the Unconscious is the part of ourselves, and the collective, that we do not have conscious awareness of, but it leads and guides many of our thoughts and actions – the goal of psychotherapy for Carl was to make the unconscious conscious so that we might direct more of our actions from a conscious space as opposed to an unconscious one (Jung, 1978, 1981). The panopticon of knowledge is present like the watchtower in and across the canons of knowledge throughout the academy presented as the necessary, unchallengeable, foundations of thought. There came a time when not only the guard within the watchtower, but also the watchtower itself, stopped being considered a watchtower at all and found its way into the unconsciousness of the subjects of the university and beyond. The Eurocentric knowledge-validation process now operates as a silent disciplinary force that is continuously reproduced and reconstituted by those committed to the continuation of the university. This system is articulated through teaching, grading systems, and, as discussed earlier, through shame. The question then becomes not how do we decolonise the discipline, or how do we decolonise the university – but instead how do we challenge the colonial overseer within ourselves? Coloniality is not separate from any one of us. If the first question of any decolonial proposition is not to uncover the coloniality and disciplinary forces within oneself, then the foundation of the exploration is inherently flawed. Even the work I am doing within this book, I know, is still deeply flawed and incomplete. The colonial overseer within me is still at work, and so I continue to do my best to find the space of fugitivity within myself and to escape the confines of my own mind, and the desire for validation and acceptance within the academy.

Many are unable to even conceive of a possibility in which knowledge may be created and exist beyond the scientific method. Here within lays the extent of our disciplined selves through the regulatory and suppressing force of the colonial panopticon that exists within so many of us. To even consider that science does not touch every edge of knowledge is to be almost blasphemous. I have found that the harsh gaze of panoptical discipline has required me to work hard in order to stay true to myself and in intellectual integrity with who I am. The panopticon of knowledge is essentially the proverbial bricks and mortar that the university is made up of. As much as a physical site of higher education the university is, it is also within itself a belief system – a philosophical tradition in consistent reproduction. It is incumbent on all of us committed to a better world to challenge and confront how we may have adopted and adapted to harmful aspects of this belief system.

The panopticon was designed to not only have the function of ensuring that prisoners did not escape, but also the function of ensuring no prisoner was able to vacate their cell to harm another prisoner. In this way the panopticon can be viewed as a site of safety as much as it can be viewed as a site of discipline. The thing that is keeping you incarcerated can also be the thing that we may end up affectionately considering as the thing we owe our lives to. This can to an extent be understood as a form of the widely popularised theory developed by Swedish criminologist and psychiatrist Niles Bejerot (1921–1988) – Stockholm Syndrome. Acknowledging the severity of the cases Stockholm Syndrome is traditionally related to, there is still something to learn here about how we may come to perceive what is actually harmful to us with affection, and at times even indebtedness. I have heard too many times across the Academy academic's commitment to the university and the disciplines whilst still speaking with a decolonial or anti-racist framework. The unwillingness for so many from any side of the political or intellectual spectrum to level any critique against the foundations of the institution for me is a reflection of the ways the panopticon of knowledge not only disciplines, but how it also allows one to feel safe. The disciplinary boundaries of the organisation of knowledge within the institution allow one to feel safe. The certainty of the payslip at the end of the month for tenured academics allows one to feel safe. The certainty of the institution – no matter the integrity – performs as a site of safety for so many in an uncertain world. However, it is through the passage of finding peace in uncertainty and chaos that we may come to know a better world – to suspend our security in mind and in body to open ourselves up to formations of knowledge, and of self, that are less linear, and instead more chaotic.

Knowledge Is Chaos

I was always taught that knowledge is something that exists outside of each of us. That a pursuit of knowledge is to find and capture truths that are timeless and unalterable. That truth exists as a constant outside of you and me, and the role of a scholar is to find that truth and articulate it just in the way it was arguably found – objectively. There is an essence of safety when thinking of the world in this way – a safety in the certainty of what has been and that we may one day know all that will ever be. That there is order, that things can be understood and grasped in their entirety by the capacity of the human mind. This is the learnt arrogance of our culture.

Knowledge defined as facts, information, or even experience is a limited way to express the vast phenomenon that is knowledge. I like to look at knowledge through a more chaotic lens. Knowledge is chaos. We can never truly know anything with absolute undeniable certainty – all knowledge, or what is considered facts, right from social phenomena to the hard sciences, is arguably contingent on this canonical model being shaped and working as it is. There are multiple and infinite possibilities of knowledge and truth; knowledge is not as all-encompassing as we are taught.

Knowledge is chaos. I offer this statement as a way to think of chaos outside of a lens of fear. The reaction when hearing a word such as chaos is often to imagine a number of negative connotations, for instance pain, suffering, or even violent war. This relates to the State of Nature discussion earlier and that Thomas Hobbes defined as a State of War – that to be ungoverned and undisciplined is to be constantly trapped in a cycle of violence and pain. Instead, I want us to consider how we might make chaos a friend. How might we work with the energy of chaos to better understand and shape the world? How does chaos offer us agency and a liberatory lens through which to see the world and ourselves?

Knowledge as chaos means that knowledge is messy, it's not linear, it comes from all and many directions, it has no beginning nor end, it is shaped and reshaped then shaped again, it is unstable, it can be conflicting, it is changeable, it is not outside of us, it resides and rises up within each and every one of us. It is both within and without. Knowledge is everywhere and in every moment being created across the planet, across the vast cosmos and beyond . . .

7

Identity and the Possible

Reclaiming the Right to Imagine

An irony I often find in the world is that we are in a continual process of demanding rights-based freedoms, though we scarcely recognise the limitations we have related to the right to *imagine*. The childlike imagination that is forcibly taught out of us through society, and specifically the schooling system, is the very imagination we require for our liberation. I sometimes question myself, and ask am I too naive? Is my thinking simply wistful impossibilities? Am I too hopeful about our collective futures? But I truly believe anything is possible. The adult mind reminded me of the logical basis of this truth, in that everything that exists in this world was first born out of the imagination of someone. So why is the expanse of my imagination, and the imagination of my peers, any different from the impact of the imagination of the forefathers of the modern world? Why should it have any less power to change the world? Why can't the world be transformed once again (and again, and again, and again)? All systems were at one point created; it then follows that at some point they may too fall. Nothing is infallible. With this, each day I give myself the permission to dream and have committed my life to supporting others through that process of returning to the imagination that has been shamed out of so many of us in a society bereft of hope. The same borders the world has constructed around nation-states to arbitrarily box and confine people in a specific land – borders that do not exist in terms of concrete reality but were born out of the imagination of a few, and are collectively reproduced in the minds and imaginations of the masses – are the same as the borders that have been constructed around our imaginations. To move towards freedom and liberation, one of the first tenets of our work must be to heal and reconcile our connection to our own imaginations.

In a liberal democracy, rights-based justice provided by the legal system can too often be the ends of our politics. Whether that be the right to marry as LGBTQ+ people, the right to bear arms, the right to have reproductive autonomy over one's body, the right to reside in a chosen country. Rights are based on a system that requires us to appeal to the sensibilities of those with power and alter the system based on single-issue struggles, though, as Audre Lorde rightly proclaimed in her address to Harvard University entitled 'Learning from the 60s', 'there is no such thing as a single-issue struggle because we do not live single-issue lives' (BlackPast, 2012b). When we place a lens on justice that allows us to view our power and potential only through a single-issue rights-based approach, there is only so far we will get. It is the surest way to continually find ourselves in a struggle as when one rights-based freedom is addressed, we are sure to have to move on to the next injustice and campaign to the powers that be for that to be overturned and the perpetual, and exhausting, cycle continues. This, I argue, is because we are falsely taught an illusion that there are some anomalous issues within our system that can be corrected if we fight hard enough. That when this issue is resolved the rest of the system does not change – because the issue was not with the system – it was with this single issue that is presented to be isolated and so no challenge to the system at large is necessary.

Conversely, the harm that is considered an inconsistency within the system is the system functioning exactly as it was designed to. Thus, it is fair to make the case that Equality, Diversity, and Inclusion (EDI) work is fallacy work if the ends we believe it will serve are freedom and liberation. It cannot offer the ends of freedom and liberation because it is based on including people on the margins into the current workings of an unjust society and does very little to challenge the roots and deep structures we are being included into. Still, Sara Ahmed's extensive work on diversity serves to shed light on some value in this type of work, specifically in *On Being Included: Racism and Diversity in Institutional Life* (2012, pp. 173–4), Sara concludes:

> I want to offer a different way of thinking about the relationship between knowledge and transformation. Rather than suggest-ing that knowledge leads (or should lead) to transformation, I offer a reversal that in my view preserves the point or aim of the argument: transformation, as a form of practical labor, leads to knowledge. The very labor of transforming institutions, or at least aiming for transformation, is how we learn about institutions as formations.

In this she offers diversity work as a phenomenological practice – that through the process of *aiming* to change institutions, knowledge about those institutions is created. The use of 'aiming' to transform is important here, because I have found that much of the knowledge created in this quest to transform institutions is knowledge of the incapacity of transformation there actually is within them. Sara uses the metaphor of a brick wall to describe this as many of her participants spoke to the blocks and limitations placed on their ability to effect change within these institutions. From my own experience of doing diversity, and even attempting decolonial, work within the institution, this proverbial brick wall was something I continued to come up against. I do question how much more knowledge we must create about institutions and what is the cost of that knowledge production. There have been a number of studies conducted on burnout in EDI practitioners, which continually find that the levels of burnout and workplace stress within these individuals is high across the board (Woods, 2022; Pemberton and Kisamore, 2023). When do we release the objective of creating knowledge about the institution at the cost of so many – and recognise the institution as incapable of meeting the demands and requests of this work? The institution is principally founded within structures that are contrary to the aims of EDI work. As mentioned, the university cannot be decolonised because it is inherently colonial. For the university to be decolonised, the university would cease to exist. So, when do we do away with the phenomenological practice that leads us to understand institutions as formations, and instead render the institution obsolete?

Still, there is a conflict within me that too acknowledges that as long as institutions are alive, EDI work is important to ensure that people on the margins experience some level of liveability within the structures of institutions – thus it is important to understand institutions as formations. This, however, is to say that the work is about marginalised people surviving within institutions as opposed to their liberation, though it is important to be clear about this differentiation. With this, EDI as a form of liberatory work is indeed fallacy work, and it is also important to recognise that even this level of liveability or survival is too often not experienced by the people who have taken on the labour of trying to make the institution more liveable as they often experience backlash and the burnout discussed above. Fundamentally, the ends of the work will not serve to end the problem; there may be some short reprieve, but this only lasts as long as the issue finds a way to morph and represent itself, albeit in a different form, because the root of the problem has not changed. It is similar to adding beautiful vibrant fresh fruits from all over the world to a fruit bowl that has a rotten piece down at the bottom – it will cover up the issue for some time – maybe even fool people enough to believe that the bowl is filled with a fresh vibrant harvest throughout. But quickly the rest of the fruit will become rotten because the foundation that it was introduced to was already putrid. In the same way, I do not want to settle for being included, or seen as an equal, within a system and society which is inherently unjust. We must believe something else is possible, that the world can be transformed, and we all have a stake in that transformation.

This is precisely why we must reclaim the right to imagine – it is not enough to paper over the cracks in a system deeply rooted in injustice. We must claim the right to imagine alternative ways of occupying the planet and forming societies and communities. For me, there is no right more important than our right to imagine – because without that we have no ability to even conceive of what true freedom and liberation may look like. The right to imagine allows us to move from a foundation of possibility, not restriction. Where we can begin to imagine just how expansively we can bend the world in the most marvellous ways – pull timelines in directions only thinkable in the quantum realm – assert a new regime of truth and possibility. As such, fiercely and unapologetically claiming the right to imagine is the core of undisciplined scholarly commitment.

From the Standpoint of Possibility

So, if I am to propose that EDI work is fallacy work, then how might identity be used in a generative way to support liberation and not just survival? For me, this is connected to exploring justice through a lens that prioritises possibility on the basis of identity and not only viewing identity as a space requiring protection. This is to say that much of the focus on identity has emanated from a space of recognising the harms that marginalised people experience – this is of course for very good reason. However, I argue that this then leads us to a space of limitation in that we guard and protect against the ills beset upon our identities and this requires so much time and capacity that it doesn't allow us to move from a more generative and possibility-orientated space.

To put this another way, what I mean is that if the game of identity was a basketball match, we have been playing defensive tactics since the inception of thinking through marginalisation with an identity lens. We have been focused on what we are against – we have been focused on anti-racism, anti-classism, queer and trans inclusion. It has been a limited game in that we are simply doing our best to not be harmed by a society that is set upon keeping us marginalised. So, if we think of oppression as the ball and to get it in the net is to cause harm to marginalised folk, we can understand that for so long our game strategy has been to do our best to play a defensive game and block the advances of the dominant culture. However, as we all know, a game played entirely in the defensive mode is not a game likely to be won. On one level it even psychologically suggests that we, the marginalised, view our opponents as the better players and better team. Our strategy has been to limit how much we lose, as opposed to advancing up the court and playing an offensive game that firmly advocates for our identities from a space of possibility. To play on the offensive is to not look at identity through the lens of protection alone, but to recognise it as a space of epistemic beauty and possibility. I often remark that nothing in life has taught me more than the experience of being a transgender person existing in a liminal space of gender amongst many intersections. My trans identity is not just an identity I want to protect, though this is the foundational tenet to ground space for possibility, but it is an identity that teaches me about hope, about transformation, about the natural world, about the complexity of human beings, about softness, about love. With this, I want to recognise that the playing of the defensive strategy of identity politics is precisely the reason I now have the ground to stand upon and reckon with the possibilities of my gender and other identities. As such, this is not to diminish the work of EDI and other strategies for supporting the rights and protection of marginalised communities. But it is to say that we must now also give ourselves permission to advance and open up our imaginations to engage with identity through more lenses than one.

Equality, Diversity, and Inclusion work arose as a response to the recognition and growth of the field of identity politics. The term *identity politics* was coined in the seminal Combahee River Collective Statement in 1977 wherein a collective of African American women came together to write a manifesto based on knowledge produced from their lived experiences (BlackPast, 2012a). This statement is also considered one of the earlier written expressions of intersectionality, the way systems of oppression affecting Black women work together to form a unique interlocking experience, a term later offered by Kimberle Crenshaw's (1994) essay entitled 'Mapping the margins: intersectionality, identity politics, and violence against women of color'. In defining the term *identity politics*, the Combahee River Collective Statement authors wrote:

We realize that the only people who care enough about us to work consistently for our liberation are us. Our politics evolve from a healthy love for ourselves, our sisters and our community which allows us to continue our struggle and work. This focusing upon our own oppression is embodied in the concept of identity politics. We believe that the most profound and potentially most radical politics come directly out of our own identity, as opposed to working to end somebody else's oppression.

Here, the authors firstly outline that their politics evolve from love. This is a deeply radical and until this point largely untouched relational point in intellectual circles. To have a politics grounded in love seems somewhat antithetical to political strategies prevalent across capitalist societies dominating the Global North, as within our societies the emotional world is often disregarded when considering political strategy in favour of a solely empiricist view related to economy and geopolitics, though I believe there is no greater political strategy than love, and I will explore this in more depth in the concluding chapters of this book. It was from this space of love that the Combahee River Collective theorised, which led them to developing a politic that focused on defining and challenging their own oppression. It was due to the work of Black women like those of the Combahee River Collective, and so many more, that we have seen such strides in efforts towards anti-oppression in all its forms. It is because of these Black women that I have been able to think and move through the world in the ways that I do, though where my own love politic of radical work now leads me is not to focus only on ending my own oppression. As discussed, my love ethic also leads me to focus on what the liberatory possibilities of my specific identity are. This is a very subtle yet incredibly important nuance that must be understood.

The power and the legacy of identity politics as defined by the Combahee River Collective cannot be understated; it has given me the keys to rooms that were firmly locked otherwise, it has given me language and frameworks to understand my own lived experiences of oppression which allowed me to do the necessary work to develop strategies to combat that oppression. Still, as time has elapsed, I would also argue that it is incumbent on us as the new generation of thinkers, activists, and world-benders to develop the theories of those that have come before us. In this vein, identity politics was designed in light of a response to oppression and so, as discussed, largely focuses on the phenomenological process of defining and then rooting out our own oppression. Whilst this is such critical work, and what has guided so much of both my intellectual and activist work over the past decade, what I have become incredibly interested in is the somewhat different phenomenological practice of understanding our identities as a location of possibility and potential, as opposed to understanding identity politics as the vehicle to root out our oppression alone. This is not to say that those who work with identity politics do not have a vision of a collective future based in imagination and liberation; instead it is to say that here I want to develop that direct relationship between identity and imagination which I feel has been largely under-theorised, potentially on the basis that it is taken as an implicit assumption. R.D.G. Kelley's (2022) work in *Freedom Dreams: The Radical Black Imagination* was a much-needed break in this as a clear demonstration of the relationship between identity and possibility. As well as work in the space of speculative and visionary fiction such as that of writers like adrienne maree brown, Alexis Pauline Gumbs, and Walidah Imarisha to name a few. Still, I feel that there is much work to do in this arena and it is incumbent on all of us committed to liberation to make the relationship between possibility and identity abundantly explicit, and *theorise* it deeply with intention and clarity.

With this, I recognise that it is a great blessing that protecting myself from oppression does not need to be the first tenet of my politics at this moment. Much work has been done by those who have gone before me that I do not need to have a limited response to oppression – I can now move into the space of possibility. This is because the decades of transformative work that identity politics has influenced has created an environment where I, and so many, feel somewhat safe enough to dream and vision beyond this world and are able to incorporate the location of our identities as central to the foundation of this radical dreaming. So, instead of responding to an oppressive world, we can utilise the concept Patricia Hill

Collins (1996) explores in her paper 'The social construction of Black feminist thought', of 'epistemic privilege' to ground our connection to the possible. This is the acknowledgement that in areas concerning one's own oppression the oppressed have epistemic privilege to create knowledge about that reality and experience. In line with this thesis, I would argue that epistemic privilege stretches beyond defining our own oppression and into a privileged vantage point to define the possible. This is to say, the oppressed *must* be the authors of the future, and it is incumbent on all of us not only to define our own oppression but to recognise the epistemic privilege this offers us in relation to recognising why and how the world needs to be bent, as well as just how much transformation is possible. Identity politics is not only a discursive tool; it stands at the vanguard of the possible.

This is also to clarify that I do not believe that the end of oppression leads to liberation; something more is required. There is a different quality in experience of an ends that is constitutive of a negation of oppression, as opposed to an embodied experience of liberation. That if the sole focus of our politics is the reactive journey to stop oppression, we are saying only what we are against, not what we are for. So, this is why it is important to dream and play with the possible and recognise the value the standpoint of our identities offers us in this journey. With this, there has been great healing value in the process of understanding my identity and giving language to the experiences of what it has meant to exist at the axes of oppression I inhabit. bell hooks (1994) writes in *Teaching to Transgress*:

> I came to theory because I was hurting – the pain within me was so intense that I could not go on living. I came to theory desperate, wanting to comprehend – to grasp what was happening around and within me. Most importantly, I wanted to make the hurt go away. I saw in theory a location for healing.

Theory has been more than an intellectual project for me; it has consistently been an emotional, psychological, and embodied process of a route to better understanding myself and healing deep wounds that I have incurred through living in the social world. The healing potential of theory began for me in understanding and giving language to my lived experiences of oppression and it now extends deeply into the healing I experience through theorising about the possibilities that emanate from the location of my own identity. It is with great joy I explore the unique vantage points that an embodied experience of the complexities of the fullness of my identity offer me. The enchanting and expansive life of a Black trans person living in a liminal space of gender, with dyslexia and dyspraxia that allow me to think in gorgeously imaginative and radical ways because my mind was not created in a neurotypical way, throttled from what we call 'Endz' – an uncompromisingly working-class upbringing in South London, UK – into the hallowed halls of Cambridge, my work and research were always going to be outside of the box. My identity is with me everywhere I go, it offers me the lens for everything I see, and it shapes my unique perspective on how we create a better world. I am grateful, profoundly grateful, for my identities because they glisten a guiding light onto a path less travelled, and from this space I am able to uncover and retrieve knowledges to share with the collective so that what is unseen for so many can become seen. It is for this reason that embracing and recognising our identities and understanding them as the lens through which we experience the world is so crucial to being an Undisciplined Scholar.

8

Trans(cendent) Epistemologies

Queerness is a longing that propels us onwards . . . Queerness is that thing that lets us know that this world is not enough, that indeed something is missing.

(Munoz, 2009, p. 1)

Queerness is a rupture in space and time. It disrupts the boundaries between impossible and possible, between right and wrong, between pleasure and pain. For this reason, the lens of queerness has much to teach us about undisciplining epistemologies. A standpoint of deep epistemic value that I believe has been greatly under-theorised in its radical potential is that of being transgender. As a trans person it often feels we are under such consistent and painful attack from the media, from the medical institution, from friends and family, and even at times from ourselves that to grant the space for trans possibility and trans dreaming feels superfluous. However, I believe that this is critical work both for our wellbeing, and for the greater collective journey to holistic liberation. Here I explore specifically the powerful and transformative knowledge held in the experiences of transgender people, and what this has to teach us about the production of knowledge. I believe that within this lens and standpoint of transgender experiences there is, laid dormant, a powerful framework of knowledge production that all can learn pertinent truths from, and which has the potential to move us closer to collective liberation and freedom.

Undisciplining Gender

There was such power in seeing someone break the rules and, rather than be punished for it . . . be applauded for it; in watching David bathe in, rather than run from, the knowledge that he was going against expectations.

(Alabanza, 2022, pp. 70–1)

Here – my dear friend and non-binary artist, writer, and performer Travis Alabanza is reflecting in their debut memoir, *None of the Above: Reflections on Life Beyond the Binary*, on the ways David Hoyle – a British avant-garde performance artist – uses the stage as a site of undisciplined, rule-breaking, gender-bending exploration. I am interested in what it means to lean into the incongruencies of life, to break the rules that have been hammered into us to keep us in line. This rule-breaking is often the art of living for those of us that live outside of the gender binary. Conversely, academia thrives on these kinds of rules, on processes, on well-tested and empirically provable routes of enquiry. Methods are the processes through which we create strategies to come closer to knowing – we isolate variables and observe phenomena in an effort to *know*. To know beyond reasonable doubt that something sits comfortably at a single end on the binary between true and false – between fact or fiction. It is seen as almost common sense within the academy to value and validate these traditional static methods and modes of inquiry as more legitimate than those which may sit outside of these strict boundaries.

I often question why these binaries exist – yes, the empirical argument is part of this conversation – it is helpful to know things from an empirical standpoint so we can navigate life in a way that is safer and with more understanding. But what happens when phenomena cannot be defined through empiricism? Do we immediately place it at the false or fictitious side of the binary? Do we always need to convince a scholarly community of phenomena in order to accept them as true, or even possible, within our society? This is based on the assumption or belief that truth is something that exists outside of ourselves – that truth is something that is constant and can objectively be observed by others. To be trans is to defy this logic. In this logic the scientist should be able to find some biological or gene-related reason for transgender identities. Given this has not been found to be possible – other than arguably for those who identify as both trans and intersex – it would follow that trans people are either all liars, or we simply do not exist. There is something so critical and powerful that is in the fabric of being trans or existing beyond the binary that requires us to engage in the art of truth-making, world-bending, and world-making in ways that a scholarly community cannot validate through the scientific method.

Of course, there have been numerous concerning studies to attempt to find something within the genetic make-up of people to give concrete evidence for homosexuality or trans identities. However, as mentioned no gene formation has been found to identify this, and it is reasonable to doubt that one ever will be found. But more importantly, I reject the notion that any scientific evidence or proof that we cannot help but be queer or trans is required or even desirable. I wonder whether scientific evidence would offer the validation that some parts of the community so ardently desire, or whether it would in turn become a mechanism for further policing and further atomisation of our communities. Beyond this, there is just something so beautiful and expansive that exists in the space of wonder held open when science is unable to define and explain phenomena. This space of wonder is something Travis also beautifully explores throughout *None of the Above*, by offering what it means to live a life that defies, even triumphs over, the gender binary. They explore both the difficulties that are experienced in such a life but also, so profoundly, the possibilities, beauty, and freedoms that exist in gender-fuckery. We are offered a window into understanding their experience and how they have come to be in a consistent practice of validating their own truth, creating their own epistemological model, in a world and knowledge system that continues to delegitimise and invalidate their identity.

As a person that also lives beyond the binary, I believe that my truth does not become any truer through the validation of evidence gained as a result of the scientific method. Nor does it have some guaranteed beneficial outcome for my communities. I have found ways and grounds to validate myself and craft an apparatus of truth in the universes I live in through alternative methods to those which dominate the presiding knowledge system. This makes me think of a documentary I watched before I came into my identity as trans. It was about the Dogon People of Mali, who knew truths science was unable to capture until centuries later (HISTORY, 2023; Science Channel, 2023). Now writing about it, I wonder how much this alternative route to gaining knowledge that I witnessed in the Dogon people influenced my own ability to believe my truth even if science would not legitimate it to me. The documentary explored how the Dogon people, who believe they descended from the Sirius star system, have a ritual that takes place every 60 years called the Sigui wherein they re-enact the movement of the star system through ritual dance. The documentary explores that the Dogon people have held the knowledge of the movement of the Sirius star system, and particularly the existence of the star Sirius B, prehistorically. It was not until the 1860s that Western science and technology was able to build a telescope strong enough to be able to observe Sirius B and its movements in the skies. This advance for Western science confirmed that the Dogon's knowledge of the Sirius star system was correct – the Dogon people had commented on its gravitational pull, the shape of the orbit, and density of the star (*Dogon Cosmology*, 2011). Further, Malidoma Patrice Somé, a well-renowned author and spiritual leader of the Dagara people of Burkina Faso, remarked in a 1993 interview with *M.E.N.* magazine that the Dogon people are some of the greatest astrologers of all tribes and within the Dogon the great astrologers are often 'gay' (Hoff, 2014). Reading the piece and what the Dagara have broadly written about gay people, whom they call the Gatekeepers, as neither the terms gay and lesbian nor transgender exist within Dagaran culture, they are thought to be those that 'stand on the threshold of the gender line. They are mediators between the two genders' (Somé, 2000). I believe it is fair to assume that to them this includes, or arguably is even more aligned with, gender-variant and trans people, though the language they had access to defining this through was that of sexuality.

I often remark that nothing has taught me more in this life-time about what is possible and the benefits of rule-breaking, than being trans and existing beyond the binary. Nothing has affected me to seek knowledge of self – and truths beyond anything that is provable – than being trans. We live in a world that teaches us we are wrong, or at best misguided, when we emerge with knowledges of ourselves that are yet to be validated and proven by the scientific method. The consequence of this is the rampant transphobia within societies across the world. The relationship between the emerging dominance of the scientific method and queer and transphobia is critical to understand. There are a mass of oral histories, and literature, that can be found which explore the role trans people played in communities prior to colonisation in lands formerly colonised (Somé, 2000; Bolich, 2007; Hoff, 2014). Still, beyond this, it is not just the fact that we existed prior to colonisation that is important here; it is also the fact that there was no static, immovable, reductive method that created a taxonomy of knowledge in the same way the scientific method and its dominance has done so today. Thus, the salvation is found less so in the fact that we were present, and have always been here, but more so in the existence of a knowledge system that was not founded upon and entrapped by binary thinking. Autonomy over oneself was valued, and there was collective trust that knowledge of self is a location of valid knowledge production that should be embraced. However, the taxonomy of knowledge we exist within deems anything that cannot be legitimated clearly through science, or simply outside of ourselves, as something deserving of exclusion and reproach. This is something this text offers an alternative to, and this can be demonstrated through the lens and experiences of the trans community.

Trans Epistemology

Trans and queer people have complicated and thrown into contestation what it means to know. Perhaps my position of writing as a trans person – as a queer, Black, neuro-diverse trans person – has had the most pronounced impact on the way I approach both life and the academy. As discussed, in the academy we often focus on the material consequences of these identities and how they shape marginality in the material world. But I have for quite some time now been more interested in these identities as categories of possibility rather than marginality. The offering of queer methodologies (Nash and Browne, 2010; Browne *et al.*, 2017; Compton, Meadow, and Schilt, 2018) began to formulate my understanding and relationship to the expansiveness of my identity as not just a product of marginality but as a mode and method through which I live and understand the world. Jack Halberstam (2018, p. 13), a seminal queer theorist, defines queer methodology as

> a scavenger methodology that uses different methods to collect and produce information on subjects who have been deliberately or accidentally excluded from traditional studies of human behavior. The queer methodology attempts to combine methods that are often cast as being at odds with each other, and it refuses the academic compulsion toward disciplinary coherence.

Here in his critical work *Female Masculinity*, Jack describes queer methodologies as undisciplined, in that they give space for methods that do not always sit alongside each other to be patchworked together to create something that a traditional approach to methods and methodology may reject. This is the art of queering – to disrupt and renegotiate what can be held and experienced through one body, and in this case one *body* of knowledge. Stacey Waite (2015) consolidates this in her article 'Cultivating the scavenger: a queerer feminist future for composition and rhetoric', wherein she explores the value of writing into contradictions and confusion as opposed to stifling the textured, complex, and complicated realities that structure the life of queer folk. She writes (2015, pp. 65–6):

> There is something queer about writing – something indescribable, something contradictory, something, at times, dare I say impossible to 'teach' in the traditional ways . . . This inevitably means we will need to misbehave, to disobey our own disciplinary rules, to push the boundaries of what we think we already know.

Here Stacey is offering a lens into the lived realities of queer folk in that us moving into our true identities can at times be seen as us misbehaving and even disobeying figures such as our parents, our communities, even at times the law – but that disobedience is what is required to simply live. The laws and social frameworks prevalent in the world are structures that some of us cannot help but spill out of, structures that some of us cannot help but need to climb and escape from. To be queer, and to be trans, is to be in a space of fugitivity. To escape the confines of societal expectation and to take the risk to build a home for oneself, and one's community, in spaces of liminality, uncertainty, and exclusion. But what happens in these fugitive spaces can be the eruption of the greatest joys and freedoms, as we witness in spaces shaped for queer communities across the world such as the ballroom, community groups, and the dancefloor. In these spaces of fugitivity, being and becoming are experienced and witnessed; new knowledges are formed and sculpted. Stacey and Jack offer a comprehensive understanding of queer methodology in that it is the coming together of what is seemingly contradictory and crafting narratives from the confusion – I feel there is something exceptionally beautiful and even erotic about this bringing together of the unfamiliar, the outlawed. From this space of the erotic Audre Lorde (2013) teaches us that knowledge is formed and shaped. With this she discusses the erotic as a 'source of power and information' (p. 54). Audre describes the erotic as the 'nurturer or nursemaid of all our deepest knowledge' (p. 56), that is to say that the erotic not only serves a function of sexuality and desire, but it is also the place within ourselves that we have access to *know*, to discover our deepest truths. The erotic is not based on logic, nor is its foundation in the material world of empirical truths – the erotic is a resting place within us all, filled with deep feeling, desire, and knowledge for which we can call to rise up and teach us 'non-rationalist' truths that are beyond science and the logics of the material world.

The lens of the erotic offers a reversal in which it lays a ground for knowledge and knowing to be found within us as opposed to outside of us. This look inward for knowledge and truth is the foundation of what I propose as *trans epistemology*. To be trans is to look at the scientific nature of your own physical body and to say that there is a deeper truth within yourself that comes from a space that science cannot detect. That truth says this body is not correct, or that this body is not an extension of my inner knowledge, or this body's expression must be different from what I am told is *right* or the norm. It is to see the gender marker on your birth certificate, to go through years, and in many cases decades, being socialised and told you are x gender beyond any reasonable doubt but to find a glimmer of spaciousness for oneself in which that becomes defiable. To sculpt and craft a space of possibility on a blackened canvas of immovable scientific 'fact', that is the gorgeous wondrous journey of what it means to be trans.

Trans epistemology is intricately related to queer methodologies in that it requires this connectedness between unthinkable contradictions, but it takes the ideas beyond the pairing and expression of the contradictory ways of coming to know into an alternative way of coming to know altogether. Trans epistemology is both about piecing together the contradictory and incoherent, but it is also about creating from absolute nothingness what is not on the table. What I mean by this is that to be trans is to move into this void of darkness, of nothingness, and from this space one must imagine and cultivate what is considered an impossibility. It is the process of birthing a new being into the world, sculpted through the eye of one's own profound imagination. To be in the consistent, insubordinate, and marvellous process of creating oneself into being each day.

To be trans has taught me that nothing is impossible. It has taught me that if in this short lifetime I have lived I can transform this much, that then the world too can transform in unimaginable ways. It is, and will continue to always be, my flame of undeniable hope. It has taught me that the truth that exists within me is my greatest resource in this world, and it is incumbent on me to not fall into the darkness of a limiting and finite world when the infinite is both possible and desirable. It has taught me that time is not as linear and fixed as I once thought it was – it has taught me that I can shift and bend and shape, and then reshape again time and temporality. To witness myself in different stages of my life as both Black woman and Black man, and neither, and all. To have pulled in a timeline in which I am able to live as my truest self, against the harsh backdrop of a possible timeline in which I lived within the confines of the limiting imagination I know so many wanted me to live out. I self-published an article reflecting on these very sentiments in 2020 entitled 'One year on testosterone: time, spirituality, and the (un)gendering of Blackness' (Owusu, 2020). Here is an excerpt from that piece that encompasses this notion of trans epistemology:

> To me, my transition is both a fugitive rupture within, and a reclamation of, time. What does it mean for me to be able to sculpt my own genealogy of self, to not be told that I must exist at one binary side of a spectrum to be valid? I have chosen, in a queer black radical act of self-definition, to personally divest from the narratives of complete 'death' of self that undergird the medical model of transition. I choose to not leave all parts of myself behind, to reclaim my inner child in all of her fullness and give her all of the love and care she deserved. To assert that integrating my past into my present and my future no less validates who I am, and who I was . . .
>
> Still, I stand in the Wake of my former self; I grieve her not because she has died but because I am too oft told I must leave her behind. That is why I am committed to living my life as spiritual speculative fiction – as so many black people that have come before me have done to survive – and to live. To imagine something in my mind and spirit that does not exist in the current mass imagination, but something that has existed in my ancestors – freedom. I think of Hortense Spillers conception

of the ungendering of black flesh, I think of C. Riley Snorton's (2017) examination of ungendering and trans capability as a sight of fugitivity and a mechanism for Black people to gain their freedom in the antebellum South, (p. 59):

> The ungendering of blackness became a site of fugitive manoeuvres wherein the dichotomized and collapsed designations of male-man-masculine and female-woman-feminine remained open – that is fungible – and the black's figurative capacity to change form as a commoditized being engendered flow ... being in a world where gender – though biologized – was not fixed but fungible, which is to say, revisable within blackness, as a condition of possibility.

To think of gendering and ungendering as a category of possibility and transformation is the work and the life I commit to living. To draw on the knowledge, power, and vision of our collective ancestors to find the ability to imagine and traverse reality. This is the Wake Work Christine Sharpe (2016) spoke of, a wake being a 'ritual through which we enact grief and memory ... a mode of inhabiting and rupturing this episteme with our known lived and un/imaginable lives' (pp. 16–18). That whilst I stand in the Wake of my former self, I use this as a portal of (un)gendered imagination and of inspiration – an act of grief but also of memory of how I have lived in this life and how I may have lived in many others. To even approach this work viewing my body and soul as a sight through which my ancestors have inscribed many truths and many memories that I can access, not through literature or artefacts, but through spiritual rituals and connection that support my understanding of self.

Christina asks of us that 'we must be undiscipled' (p. 13), Saidiya Hartman (2019) allows us to imagine our own lives as 'beautiful experiments', to engage in her conceptualisation of the wayward or waywardness as 'insurgent grounds that enables new possibilities and new vocabularies . . . it is a queer resource of black survival'. She writes (pp. 227–8):

> Waywardness is a practice of possibility at a time when all roads, except the ones created by smashing out, are foreclosed. It obeys no rules and abides no authorities. It is unrepentant. It traffics in occult visions of other worlds and dreams of a different kind of life . . . an ongoing exploration of what might be . . . it is the untiring practice of trying to live when you were never meant to survive.

How much of ourselves do we allow to become silenced, to remain asleep or unconscious to the world? How deeply are we committed to the material and possible, that we neglect the immaterial and impossible? Giving ourselves the purest right to imagine, the right to reject and revolutionise the worlds that we live in and ourselves from the inside out. To engage in wayward beautiful experiments, to dance and imagine with our ancestors in the present and the future, to unchain and unfix ourselves from the bounds of time and of material 'reality'. What a beautiful possibility.

So, I have nothing more to leave you with than a reminder that this is just a fraction of the thoughts and feelings I have experienced over this past year on testosterone. Sometimes, I get sad that my beard is yet to connect (L), or that my body still engages in the monthly shedding of the lining of my uterus. Though I have become thankful for this body that carries me, and thankful for the pace at which my transition is going – it reminds me not to hold on to time too dearly. That my body is my body and the ways that it changes and moulds slowly into what I ask it to be is a blessed process that I am lucky enough to be the closest observer of. Love is the word and principle that underwrites all that I have explored here, love in the most expansive form of the word. I am learning new ways to love myself every day and new ways to engage in love with my community, and both my chosen and familial family. I am eternally thankful for this process that I am on, and today, just like every other day I will continue to ask myself how I can grow, how I can better love, and how I can change.

Nothing has made me question my own truth and seek ways to validate that truth more than my transition. In this world where science is king, trans people are defined as anomalies to the accepted approach of knowledge production and validation. Though embracing this inherent rule-bending and -breaking that trans folk across the world demonstrate and embody is what could allow society as a whole to morph and extend into other realms of possible hope. In order to take a lens across social justice and inequalities that do not result in the fallacy work discussed earlier in this chapter, it is pertinent to look through a lens of trans epistemology as a heuristic of deep and profound transformation. To work with trans epistemology is to work with the recognition that we must create a new being, a new world, new language and names, bodies that would have otherwise never existed without the commitment to dreaming. Trans epistemology is disruptive, it is undisciplined but it is also intuitive, it requires self-love and recognition, it derives from a space of compassion for oneself in a world that too often feels like it wants to destroy us. Trans epistemology is about moving beyond that which can be known through the looking eye; it is about connecting with a level of reality that is not perceptible through the material or scientific lens, it is about transformation beyond what the logical mind can comprehend, it is about indulging in wondrous rule-breaking possibility. Above all it is about connecting with the truth that resides inside each of us; it is an opening to shining a glistening light upon the dark uncertain path of truth and possibility.

Validating My Truth Through the Unseen

My understanding of my gender acts almost as a motif for how I approach life. The lessons within it lead and guide me to better understand and maintain hope for transformation in the world as a whole. I have offered with openness and vulnerability my body as a canvas to think through some of the most critical questions that occupy the heart of this work. This, in the same way, reflects my relationship to the forms of knowledge I am concerned with here, in that it was through my personal journey of transitioning that my desire to understand and connect with other forms of knowledge arose. This was because I had so many questions that were unanswerable in the world of form, empiricism, and 'facts'. Questions that I wanted deeper answers to that felt beyond the reach of my affective and feeling self, that is to say that the fact I *felt* I wanted to transition was not enough for me to ground my desire. Why did I feel the desire to go beyond my physical body and transform it? From where did this knowledge of self derive? How could I know who I was when nothing in the a*ctual world*, nothing about the biologised body I was born into, told me that this was the case? How can I trust myself, trust my own relationship to knowledge and truth? Trust the knowledge of my interior world?

*

In *The Spirit of Intimacy: Ancient African Teachings in the Ways of Relationships*, Sobonfu Somé (2000) explores the role of the 'Gatekeepers' within Dagaran life. As mentioned earlier, I read the Gatekeepers as people in our current society who would identify as both queer and trans. Sobonfu writes: 'the words gay and lesbian do not exist in the village, but there is the word gatekeeper. Gatekeepers are people who live a life at the edge between two worlds – the world of the village and the world of spirit ... without gatekeepers, there is no access to other worlds' (p. 132). Here Sobonfu is exploring the spiritual role of queer and trans people in the Dagara tribe, as people with a specific purpose, and ability, within the community to connect with the spirit realm. Sobonfu (2000, p. 136) goes on to write:

> Gatekeepers hold the keys to other dimensions. They maintain a certain alignment between the spirit world and the world of the village. Without them, the gates to the otherworld would be shut. On the other side of these gates lies the spirit world or other dimensions . . . Gatekeepers have the capacity to take other people to those places . . . A gatekeeper's *knowledge* is different from the knowledge of mentors and elders. This is because the elders do not necessarily have access to all gateways. The gatekeepers, on the other hand, have access to all the dimensions. They can open any gate.

This demonstrates the way in which a specific form of knowledge, of epistemology, was available to the Gatekeepers that was not accessible through the phenomenological practice of experience alone as was the knowledge of the elders. How we recognise trans epistemology begins with the phenomenological understanding of our experience of transness; however, the heart and truth of trans epistemology derives not from the experience of being trans, but instead this realm of knowing that the Dagaran speak of that trans people arguably have access to. For me, I feel that this knowledge of my trans identity came from a space almost above reality; it derived from a part of me that I can only describe as being connected to a spiritual realm. I feel that it is not only the knowledge of my gendered expression that I can access through this realm; instead, my gender was that catalyst that led me into this desire to connect with my most internal and deepest knowledge. It is also through this connection that I know in the deepest corners of my soul that transformation and liberation, beyond what I can even form into words on this page, are possible within this world.

I want to consider the proposition of the Gatekeepers as more than a historical ode that recognises that us trans folk existed prior to colonisation – instead I want to go into the Dagaran experience and look outward, as opposed to an anthropological looking from the outward in. To consider deeply that perhaps queer and trans folks have knowledges that do not derive only from the 'actual' world; instead, they have access to knowledge emanating from the spirit world(s). Knowledge which cannot be located as deriving from anywhere other than an 'elsewhere', this elsewhere being spiritual realms and dimensions, and they can gather knowledge from these other dimensions, and then express this knowledge in material reality. It is important to remember that equally all people have access to the spiritual realm in some form; the access of the Gatekeepers, for the Dagaran people, is, however, unique. This is an idea that tracks across a number of precolonial cultures, for instance the Dogon people of Mali are understood to have believed that the perfect human was androgynous (Bolich, 2007). For the Lugbara people of Uganda and the Democratic Republic of Congo, there are equally people who occupy a liminal space of gender for the purpose of connecting with the spiritual realm. The names for these people are Okule – male-to-female mediums ('like women') – and Agule – female-to-male mediums ('like men') (Middleton, 2004). Echoing this, across South Asia there are the Hijra people, in Native American communities there are two-spirit people, the list continues for communities across the world and the various names (or at times nameless) expressions of people who defy the gender binary and, with this, have a specific access to spiritual realms.

*

The question I am asked is often how did you *know*?

How did I know I was trans? How did I drown out the voices of the trans-exclusionary radical feminist (TERF) lobbies? How did I drown out the voices of friends and family? How did I do something so brave and permanent without lived experience of the outcome on the other side?

For me, the truth is, perhaps I wasn't so brave. Perhaps I did not extend myself into something I knew nothing about.

I spent days, weeks, months, years agonising over the decision. Trying to *know* if it was right for me – searching for examples of people who had lived out the experience and did not seem to regret it. But none of them were me.

The conflict continued.

It was around this time I was introduced to tarot cards, the ancient Hellenistic divination system used to share intuitive wisdom through the archetypes and energies held within the images and numerology of the cards. Something within me felt deeply drawn to these cards; I wanted to understand them, to work with them, to see if I could *know* truth differently through utilising them. I set upon the journey of studying each card, I began meditating and connecting more intentionally with nature to strengthen my relationship to my intuition. I began slowly reading for myself, and later for friends. This led me on a deep spiritual journey – after tarot I learnt to read Hellenistic birth charts, then I began learning about the Orishas of Ifá, Candomblé, and Santería, I later studied the Hermetic practice of alchemy, I erected an ancestral alter, studied the ancient art of numerology, I began taking my yogic practice very seriously both in terms of the asana (postures) and all seven other limbs of yoga. I was finding that with each of these different forms of spirituality, I felt led back to the same source, I was led back to myself. In essence, I was journeying above reality in order to harness intuitive messages and better understand myself, better relate to a truth that was inside of me – yet connected to the whole.

With this, I decided that I would use tarot to explore who I am with regard to my gender identity. I felt I knew who I was deeply within, but a part of me, the part still anchored to this reality – the part held back by fear – needed to witness something at least partially through my senses to trust my inner knowledge of self. So, in this pursuit to go above reality, I drew cards to confirm to myself my inner knowledge. To connect to an intelligence beyond my physical body, to draw in information, to draw in knowledge, knowledge located in what I can only describe as a spiritual realm. I was speculating through tarot about my gender, and it brought through strong confirmations that my inner knowing was indeed the highest way for me to progress.

In a similar vein, around the same time I started a therapeutic journey with a woman who folded spirituality into her practice. We were in a deep meditative experience wherein I was guided to invite my inner child into the room. Through the meditation I felt I extended beyond this reality into a different space of knowledge and truth outside of what I was able to locate within the 'actual' world. In this exploration of a different layer of 'my' consciousness what stood out to me was that when she asked me to invite an older version of myself into the room, I saw myself as a male-presenting person. At this time, I was struggling deeply with the idea of being male-presenting and considering only socially transitioning as non-binary. It was in this moment I knew. She asked me how the younger version of me felt with the older version – and the single word that left my lips was *'safe'*.

It is incredible to reflect in the moment, I am that person I saw in my meditation. I feel safer in myself, and in my body than I have ever felt before.

*

In an occurrence I can only describe as synchronistic, I was invited to a fully funded summer school in Salvador de Bahia, Brazil, in 2018. On this trip I was initiated more deeply into my understanding of Candomblé, the Afro-Brazilian tradition, which has its main home in the State I visited. On this journey I came across an Orisha, specific to Candomblé, called Logun

Ede. The story of Logun Ede is they are the child of Oshun, Goddess of beauty and fresh waters, and Oxossi the masculine Orisha of the forests and hunting. It is believed that Logun Ede lived six months of the year with her mother Oshun by the fresh waters, and during this time Logun Ede was a woman. The other six months would be lived with his father, Oxossi, at which time Logun Ede was a man. This demonstrated to me the presence of gender fuckery in my ancestors; it offered the possibility too of transition not having to be this linear occurrence that sits at one binary end of the gender spectrum. It allowed me to relinquish the 'I have always been x gender' narrative, and embrace a more fitting and temporally disruptive, or even destructive, version that deeply spoke to my own truth. It is through these spiritual stories developed centuries ago that I again came back to myself.

*

I travelled to Berlin a lot throughout my twenties; it was a place I felt free and deeply at ease with myself – there is just something about that city that continues to bring me peace. During a trip in my earlier twenties, I was coming to terms with my gender flux – I was beginning to dress in a way I found more affirming, and using they/them pronouns. At this time I had also begun seriously questioning gender affirmation surgery. Again, quite synchronistically, I met someone who had undergone 'top surgery' just a few months prior to our chance encounter. We spoke for hours and ended up continuing our conversation into the toilets of one of Berlin's most infamous Queer Dive bars, Silver Future. They had just told me they had had top surgery and offered to show me their chest, to which I emphatically obliged. We made our way into one of the stools where they lifted up their shirt and showed me the handsome scars along their chest. I followed up with asking them, in hopes they might help settle my own internal chaos, 'How did you *know*? How were you certain? I'm so scared.'

They said to me: 'You will never be 100% certain, that's a lie the medical model forces us into, but if you're considering it, if you're feeling that it may be right for you – you may as well try.' This, to me, spoke of a deep trust of moving into futures with no defined or certain guarantee on the other side: the ability to deeply trust our inner knowledge and move beyond the vices of logic and fears that can curtail our most expansive forms of radical imagining. I took this advice on wholeheartedly, not just as a reason to move ahead with my transition in the way I most deeply desired, but also as a way to live and to think through how we might reshape the worlds that we live in.

Perhaps this is where the power is found, not in concrete facts that measure the present and the past – but in belief – in deeply recognising our soul and spiritual selves in a world that values mind and body alone. To give epistemic value to a part of ourselves that cannot be understood via the tools of research and method that we have at our disposal as it stands. Instead, to lean deeply into these other forms of knowledge, into this space I speak of through which I was able to retrieve knowledge of who I deeply am in this world. This space may also be the space in which we find the power of collective belief, collective knowing, that another world is possible. That we do not have to settle for what is right in front of us, that we can extend our imaginations into realms above reality, and draw in profound and revolutionary knowledge that can bend and change the course of time.

That we can . . .

A Note on Grief

Where there is light, there too always will be a shadow. I do not want to frame trans experience as something that only has the potential to teach us about possibility and beauty, it too teaches us about pain and grief in equal abundance. There are also subtle, yet vital lessons held within this dimension of the trans experience which can further support us in developing this epistemological framework. To understand trans experiences, and *trans epistemology*, is to understand that with the power and beauty there is also a perpetual grieving process. That to have the light, we must also embrace the darkness. It makes me think of this sense of divine balance in all things.

Trans epistemology allows us to understand the process of world transformation as one that does not require a utopian vision of the world where we utilise our inner knowing to move us into a perfect world. It is instead a lens through which we can understand the power of transformation, with recognition that transformation is imperfect and that any form of change requires a deep presence with grief. I often think that the trans experience is framed as a linear endeavour towards the gender that aligns with us, and in this linear endeavour there is nothing that we grieve about our former selves, and if we were to grieve or miss any part of our former selves then that would invalidate us. There is of course the somewhat known grief of the friends and family we may lose, the access to spaces and freedom of safe movement around the world – there is a lot at stake in taking that leap into the unknown. However, I have spoken to many trans people, in closed spaces, about the grief in transitioning beyond our former selves. We need to hold space for this grief and recognise that two things can be true at once; we can miss what was and still know that we must become what we need to be. We share the acknowledgement that we would not return, but still there are so many painful points that we must hold space for us trans folk to grieve about our former selves, our former lives, and our former bodies.

This holds the recognition that with change we must always leave something behind. We must grant ourselves the space to grieve what has been left whilst navigating this terrain of becoming the transformed versions of ourselves. There is an expectation that when we speak of social justice or revolution, we must detest all that is present in the world as a requisite foundation of our legitimacy to move into the beyond. In my own practice I am working deeply on not thinking in these binary ways in which I must demonise or abhor the present in its entirety as legitimate grounds to move into alternative futures. My transition teaches me this is possible. To love and respect in ways what currently is, to find a certain sense of comfort in the present but knowing that a greater sense of liberation may exist in the future, as well as within.

I sat with some of my trans brothers recently and we are all at different stages in life and in transition. One has 'completed' his medical transition, one has been off of testosterone for almost two years as he is in the pursuit of becoming pregnant, and me four years into my medical transition considering future surgeries. We sat for hours talking about our journeys, how we feel, and have felt at each stage, and a word we continued coming back to was grief. That even with every hormone and surgery the medical model has to offer, we must still grieve the body we desire as it cannot function in the ways we know it should. We live knowing that our bodies will consistently shift and change, but only so much. We will never, in this lifetime at least, experience a body that is in perfect accord with who we know ourselves to be.

The grief is ever present in the beauty of change.

It teaches us that it is necessary to embrace the imperfect, the liminal spaces. As we move towards more liberated worlds, it is okay to miss and grieve parts of this world that we worked to overcome. It is okay to miss the embodied 'safety' of our known realities, whilst we wait for our nervous systems to catch up with our futures. It is okay for the futures we work towards to equally be imperfect and for us to build presence and acceptance in the eye of those worlds.

It makes me think of the Japanese concept of Wabi Sabi, which loosely translates to an acceptance of the imperfect, the transient, the unfinished.

9

A Praxis of Imagining: Learning to Love

It is my belief that the world we live in emanates from the imagination – everything that has been built, achieved, explored, from the most deplorable to the most abundant, has been conceived in the imagination. Hence, I have argued that the education system as it is functions as a tool and a system to curtail the depth and breadth of the imagination. So, in this concluding chapter I will turn my attention to how we might repatriate our imaginations – in their most wondrous, child-like, radical, and fugitive ways. The intention is to rupture the episteme (Sharpe, 2016) – to hold visions of collective liberation so eye-wateringly beautiful that to move onto that timeline of reality we must transform our own relationship to knowledge and reality itself. We must, too, transform our relationship to ourselves.

In the wake of the ruins of the excesses of a society we protest, what might we build? How do we become the people able to vision and extend our minds and our hearts into a space of visionary potential? The same consciousness that drives us to reckon with the harms of the society as it is and define what we are against is not the consciousness that will aid us in building alternative futures. In the ruins, will we have the tools to rebuild? How do we disidentify with the position an oppressive society places us in of consistent critique? How do we become the people ready to not just create repetitions of the world we currently occupy because all of our energy in the process of decolonisation has been focused on how to change the most violent increments of this society? How do we neither intentionally nor unintentionally create mirages of the injustices we have become accustomed to by virtue of the excesses of our pain, our fear, our insidious comfort?

Here, we turn our attention from the structure of the university, and of society, to the self. The question is not just how do we create new worlds: the greater question is how do we become the people able to sustain the alternative futures and liberatory dreams we speak of. My proposition is that much of this relies on a love ethic rooted in a deep knowing of ourselves, and our capacity.

In the Ruins

As I have mentioned, it is important to recognise and reckon with that, as much as we may abhor the system as it is, or certain expressions of the system, our nervous systems are in some way regulated to society as it is today. The injustices that surround us are our normal. The system is embedded within our very fabric of being. To imagine or call in a new world means that in order for us to sustain and be able to experience a world not engulfed by the ills of our present world, we *must* attune our nervous systems to the possibility of our imagined states.

I often think of the gift of hindsight, how we can look back on the world from the location we are in temporally today and say that the ills of societies gone by were awful. However, if we were to locate ourselves in some of those times, we may have partaken in the same ills we abhor today. To suggest or claim we would have had the moral virtue to pierce through any injustice of the past is to gravely misunderstand the mission of collective liberation. We must find peace with the fact that we are imperfect, and we are all in some way colluding with an unjust system. I cast my mind into the future and think about what will be seen as abhorrent that we so ardently take as normal today. Perhaps the climate movement will shift consciousness enough that our great grandchildren will look back at our generation as monsters for driving petrol or diesel cars and indulging in flights across the world. Perhaps there will be a shift in consciousness around food safety and health, those that we are the ancestors of will look back and not be able to comprehend how anyone could look the other way whilst another went hungry, or how corporations that sold food that led to health problems were ever allowed to market and advertise in the ways they do today. Perhaps . . .

The possibilities are endless but the work of being human is to navigate and negotiate the inconsistencies and imperfections of living, and of ourselves. This, however, should never lead to inertia by virtue of fear that we can never get it all right; quite the opposite, we should move because nothing is perfect, and with that freedom, we can experiment with what freedom may look, feel, and taste like.

It is vital that we engage with the work of transforming the world and transforming ourselves with deep humility and deep recognition of our own incongruencies. This is not work in which ego has a home. When we find ourselves in the ruins, who do we become? Gnashing mouths and the fear that the life we once lived has been taken from us? Or people able to hold our own imperfections and wrongdoings alongside another's and begin collectively and collaboratively building anew?

We must prepare for the ruins, the liminal space between this world and the next. The space that can extend and morph, transform and transmute our deepest fears into our greatest pleasures.

I witness and experience the desire for a new world as an erotic desire. It is a desire that rises from the passion-filled harvests of our souls. As discussed in Audre Lorde's (2013) seminal piece 'Uses of the erotic', the erotic is not just a location of sexuality, it is also 'a source of power and information' (p. 54). Audre defines the erotic as being located on a 'spiritual plane, firmly rooted in the power of our unexpressed or unrecognized feeling' (p. 53). She goes on to affirm (Lorde, 2013, p. 59):

> Recognizing the power of the erotic within our lives can give us the energy to pursue genuine change within our world, rather than merely settling for a shift of characters in the same weary drama.

In the ruins, how do we create what we have never before seen? In the ruins, how do we resist the compulsion to recreate the 'same weary drama' from a place of routine or lack of alternatives? How do we hold the flame of hope and freedom in our collective present moment? How do we get free using the power of the erotic?

The foundation of the word erotic is eros – the Greek word for love and desire. Just as with a person, desire may arise that first sparks intrigue in getting to know a mate and later down the line love may be built with time and care. I think the same is true for new visions of a world transformed – first comes a deep desire for change. We may not know exactly what this change looks like, but we know that moving towards it is what we must do. As with a mate, we work to learn the nature and the root of this desire, we then nourish and deepen this desire through the knowledge of another, as opposed to unknowingly throwing ourselves into the desire from a space of lust as opposed to love. We get to know this desire, we take our time with it, we learn to practise care, we learn to deeply know the truth and complexity of our desire, the desire of transformed futures. It is only then we can lovingly move into union with that desire with care and wholeness.

How might we sit to learn and listen to our desire for a new world? Perhaps we extend ourselves for the spiritual growth of another, as M. Scott Peck (2003) describes as the foundation of what a true love is in his work *The Road Less Traveled*. This is also the working definition bell hooks uses for what love is in her work *All About Love*. How might we work and live in a way that centres the spiritual growth of the collective, of society, of all? How might we learn how to move with desire to take us towards a true sense of love?

In accord with the pantheon of Black feminist thinkers, writers, artists, mothers, that have taught me well, I invoke love as the greatest political strategy.

To imagine we must first learn to love.

A Love Ethic

To love is to heal.
To heal is to love.

All problems that we recognise in the world do not just sit outside of us. It may seem the most expedient political strategy to locate all our pain and harm outside our own bodies, outside of our loved ones, and outside of our communities. To suggest the issue is solely the constructs of our current society, whether that be the police, the prison system, or capitalism, is to negate our own lived collusion in the harmful melodrama that is the society we collectively build and instruct. This is not to say that our collusion with the system is out of necessity alone, for instance we work with capitalism because we need to meet our basic needs and feel safe and secure, yet we still abhor the system – a well-argued stance.

Instead, the collusion I am speaking of here is the collusion of our hearts.

Within each and every one of us is pain and a level of trauma, which is the reality of living in a society such as ours. As we get older, that pain and trauma can express itself in many ways overt and covert, upon ourselves and upon another. It is not until we engage deeply in the process of healing these aspects within ourselves that we will be able to both imagine and maintain another possibility that is not just a reconstruction of the world as it is, just with different utterances and cloaks. A world truly different, a world where liberation is normal.

The reason I believe that liberation is possible, as I have defined earlier in this work, is that I believe all humans are inherently good. A lie we have been taught by the imposition of a Classical Liberal point of view, which now undergirds much of our modern world, is that all humans are self-seeking and selfish. However, it is my belief that people do harmful things, from a simple unkind gesture to geopolitical war crimes, from a space of their own traumatised and wounded self, or the collective pain-body of a people. This reflection has been echoed by Gabor Maté (*Doctor Gabor Mate: The Shocking Link Between Kindness & Illness!*, 2023), world-renowned physician and critical voice on the extended impact of trauma on the mind and body.

Love may seem like an easy political strategy, perhaps a cop out – however, that is only true for those of us that do not know how to love. It is far easier in this world to hate, to be angry at our dispossession than it is to love. What if we were to implement the non-linear thinking discussed in the last chapter and rather than aim to transform systems in linear ways through accepted mechanisms, such as campaigning and policy change, we instead looked within, we considered our own healing as not only necessary for ourselves but necessary for the healing of the world and the maintenance of just futures. As the age-old adage goes – hurt people hurt people. If this is true, then it must follow that healed people heal people.

My belief is that a deeper sense of transformation of our world and society may come from loving and healing approaches to ourselves and each other, rather than movement fuelled more by anger at our dispossession. That is not to say that anger does not have a righteous place in our work – but it is to say that it is critical that it is not the only strategy we utilise for our collective liberation. That when the fire of anger burns out after the latest egregious crime of the State that we are well resourced in other methods of transformation, that our movements do not rely on a sensationalised moment to function and to move. For me the most potent use of anger is to feel through that anger, experience it, and then alchemise it into passionate loving work towards our collective liberation.

It is imperative for each and every one of us to learn to deeply love ourselves and deeply recognise and love each other. So, the question remains, how do we love? Through my own life experiences and through the work of scholars and thinkers such as bell hooks, Audre Lorde, Sobonfu Somé, and M. Scott Peck, I have learnt deeply about the work, the practice, the discipline of loving. How it begins with the self and only from that space, a space of deep and true self-love, can we begin to conceive of truly loving another. Whether that love be romantic or, as we will discuss, in relation to love as a political strategy. I have come to believe that there are three pillars to living a life guided by a love ethic, and for me those pillars are purpose, releasing control, and the art of deeply *knowing*.

Purpose

A love ethic must begin with self. If to love is to nurture the spiritual growth of another (Peck, 2003; hooks, 2018), then to love ourselves is to nurture our own spiritual growth. Purpose may not be the most likely place to begin when considering what a love ethic may look like, but I believe it is the most pertinent. Purpose is too often conflated with capitalism and misrepresented as a tool of that system. Incredible work has taught a new generation about the deeply resistant power of rest. However, in this recognition we must not lose sight of the incredible alchemical power of work, of purposeful and fulfilling work, as a political strategy. We deeply require both.

Purpose is not labour for the sake of labour, nor is it necessarily work in the traditional sense. My belief is that the purpose of each of our lives is to do what we deeply love and be transformed by the process. This could truly be anything, but for me and I am sure for many others, this shows up in the space of creativity and our working lives. I believe there is something deeply sacred about work. Had the Black women who decided each day to tend to the labour of writing worlds in their heart into being not taken those intentional daily actions, I would feel lonelier in this world, less rooted. So, it is my duty too to choose to labour in a way that speaks to my soul, that lights me up from the deepest centre of my core, and allows one to share the light that is within the world.

Yes, unfortunately in these times capitalism has become interlaced with purpose in rather unhelpful ways. Still, this should not lead us to do away with the sacred act of work altogether because it is tied up with capital. Purpose is an ancient belief rooted in many of the wisdom traditions from across the world, and one a Black feminist love ethic also teaches us the beauty of.

In *All About Love*, bell hooks (2018) reflected that 'work that enhances our spiritual wellbeing strengthens our capacity to love' (p. 63). When we are in the process and action of feeling aligned and deeply integrated with the work we choose to do, we also increase our capacity to love and care because we are nurturing our own spiritual growth. From this location we can extend ourselves for the spiritual growth of our communities, and of the collective. bell hooks (2018, p. 62) recognised that:

Most people do not grow up learning that the work we choose to do will have a major impact on our capacity to be self-loving. Work occupies much of our time. Doing work we hate assaults our self-esteem and self-confidence.

Doing work we love creates space for us to love. Audre Lorde (2013, p. 57) echoed this understanding in 'Uses of the erotic', where she wrote:

> For once we begin to feel deeply all the aspects of our lives, we begin to demand from ourselves and from our life-pursuits that feel in accordance with that joy which we know ourselves capable of. Our erotic knowledge empowers us, becomes a lens through which we scrutinize all aspects honestly in terms of their relative meaning within our lives.

Equally, the Dagaran people of Burkina Faso placed great importance on one's life purpose. It was their belief that every child chooses a purpose before they are born. The community are then told the child's purpose during the pregnancy, and it then becomes the duty of the elders to place things in front of that child that helps them remember the purpose they chose before birth (Somé, 2000). In this work, *The Spirit of Intimacy*, Sabonfu Somé reflects on how, within Dagara communities, romance was never the foundation of an intimate relationship; instead, she reflects on romance as a Western illusion. In its place, the foundation of an intimate relationship for the people of Dagaran communities is purpose – how in accordance the life's purpose of your partner is with your own, is the true defining element of the compatibility and success of an intimate relationship. This is not to say that romance does not play a role in Dagaran unions, but it is to say that one must not seek their happiness and meaning through another and it is only from this recognition that any healthy relationship can be formed.

It is through purpose that we locate joy, we locate content-ment, we locate the truth of who we are. It is through purpose that we connect with our infinite power, it is through pur-pose that we connect with the Divine. For me, it is through purpose that I have been able to deeply heal. When it comes to creating liberated futures, I often reflect that it can be per-ceived that there is an archetypal way to do this work. That the way to 'change the world' is to work for an NGO, or grassroots organising, or to be on the frontline of each protest. These fields of work are certainly the calling of some, but to choose the work based on our perceived outcome is to dishonour our-selves and our truth. Inversely, it has the opposite impact: if we do work that does not settle our soul because for whatever reason we believe it is 'good' work, we do not give our hearts the conditions they need to flourish. The flourishing of our hearts is truly an irreplaceable tenet for moving into more just futures.

A friend whom I studied alongside during my first degree had a glint in his eyes when he imagined Pan-African futures. It was the dream of his heart, and his intellect to offer to the cause of a stronger and more self-determined African con-tinent. Equally, he had always loved the arts as a child and dreamed of taking to the stage or the silver screen. As we con-cluded our undergraduate years, he decided to take the path he witnessed as the most direct to his vision of Pan-African unity as well as financial security. This was to work for an NGO; after an extended unpaid internship he was given an entry-level role. As time went on, he realised how ineffective the organisation was at doing impactful work and began to feel restless as well as underpaid and underappreciated. During COVID he was made redundant and experienced both the grief and elation of this moment. It gave him an opening to try his hand at his childhood dreams of acting and he moved into this desire with full force. After many conversations, he reflected that he may be able to make an even greater impact in Pan-Africanist visioning if he is a successful actor and screenwriter, and in the process, he is able to do work that brings him deep joy, whilst still expanding his learning and thought around Pan-Africanism and liberation.

Sobonfu reminds us that our purpose is not always something that we move into with open arms, that fear and discomfort equally play a part in our journey towards ourselves. She wrote (2000, p. 75):

> I was reluctant to do certain things, and realized that to promise to do something before being born does not mean having the courage or the willingness to do it. The idea of leaving the village especially did not appeal to me at all. I wanted someone to delete that part of my life purpose.

To live in purpose does not mean that life will be easy at every turn, or that we will always want to do the work of our soul. But it is through that labour we become more of ourselves, and we find the beauty and joy that the journey has to offer. I wish we spoke about purpose more in movements, I wish we spoke about what lights us up and anchors our work in relation to who we are, not just the world we desire to see. In ancient Vedic traditions this concept of purpose is often referred to as living in one's Dharma. In the *Bhagavad Gita*, a central Vedic text, Krishna reminds Arjuna that (Easwaran, 2007, pp. 261–2):

> By performing one's own work, one worships the Creator who dwells in every creature. Such worship brings that person fulfilment. It is better to perform one's own duties imperfectly than to master the duties of another. By fulfilling the obligations he is born with, a person never comes to grief.

It is better to live in alignment with our own truth, to the best of our ability, than it is to try to align with someone else's.

In ancient Japanese traditions this principle is called living one's Ikigai. It is equally found in Ancient Roman Stoicism gorgeously reflected in the passage from Marcus Aurelius' *Meditations*: 'all you have to do is be attentive to the power inside you and worship it sincerely' (Aurelius, 1800, p. 24). *Purpose* preceded capitalism, and I believe it important to not allow capitalism to rob us of the vitality and ancient liberatory power of this approach to living.

Of course, capital plays a part in our ability to do work and live lives we deeply love. There is much I could write about this, though all I will say here is that when I embarked upon higher education, I had planned to become a commercial lawyer because my primary goal was to move my family out of poverty. During the final year of my undergraduate degree, one day I heard an almost audible voice that said to me 'if you do what you love, you will be exceptional at it. If you are exceptional at what you do, money has no choice but to follow.' This is now a principle I live my life by. Of course, there are times I resist out of frustration, out of fear, out of inadequacy, but slowly I find my way back to myself each time. My work in this life is to explore, indulge in, and create knowledge – the knowledge of myself and knowledges for the collective. It is to study the knowledges of communities throughout time and space and consider what they may have to teach us today. It is to create spaces for others to move deeply into the joy and liberation that is convening with other ways of knowing. It is to deeply feel and orienteer through every experience I have in this life-time and collect the lessons and scriptures I find along the way. This is how I serve community; it is also how I heal myself.

No mistakes have been made with the desires that lay within your heart. It is incumbent on each of us to search our hearts and believe in our own interior truths to live and be the people we most desire. I believe nothing is greater for society and our collective cause of liberation than to live in integrity with the calling of our souls.

When we do what we love, we create the space to love.

It is truly counterinsurgent work within a world that tries to dictate to us who we are and who we should be to listen within and follow our own compass. It is an act of radical refusal to do the work we love – to be filled with meaning, purpose, and joy each day. A radical liberatory praxis.

When people are living in alignment with their purpose and their truth, they vibrate a certain energy, an aura almost, of joy and contentment. It is as Audre writes: 'there is, for me, no difference between writing a good poem and moving into the sunlight against the body of a woman I love' (Lorde, 2013, p. 58). To create from a place of centredness is an erotic pursuit, it is life-giving not energy-sapping as much of the way we experience and view work today may seem.

The invocation is to begin thinking about purpose and work in a different way, through a different lens. Liberation does not need to look linear. Love does not need to look a certain way either. It is when we seek that knowledge of self, and are courageous enough to live it out, that we extend ourselves for the radical work of our own spiritual growth, and by extension that of the healing and growth of society as a whole.

Releasing Control

Throughout this book I have placed an emphasis on the location from which an act comes, as opposed to only the outcome of that act. In chapter 2 we explored the intention of an Undisciplined Scholar, and in chapter 7 we explored our relationship with chaos and how becoming more attuned to chaos can actually enhance our liberatory potential. It is not only the outcome that matters, but it is also the intention and the process of any act that is of equal importance. The argument against this may be that many people may have ill-guided intentions, but this is why it is important to release control. If an intention is ever to control or dominate another person, a municipality, or an outcome, then this is not an act guided by a love ethic. Intention must be grounded in a firm love ethic that honours both self, and every other being that inhabits this planet.

In *All About Love* bell hooks made clear to us all that love cannot co-exist with abuse, nor with domination. bell later reflected that one of the ideas that was really hard for people to accept from this work was that if somebody is abusing you, they are not loving you. I found myself included in those people who struggled to accept this truth. I had to reflect deeply on the ways I have tried to make sense of life by believing that abuse and love could indeed co-exist. Even if someone's intention is to love, yet they cannot release control of their own desired outcome, this is not living and engaging with a love ethic – it is domination and abuse.

bell hooks (2018, pp. 87–8) wrote:

> Awakening to love can happen only as we let go of our obsession with power and domination . . . A love ethic presupposes that everyone has the right to be free, to live fully and well. To bring a love ethic to every dimension of our lives, our society would need to embrace change . . . embracing a global vision wherein we see our lives and our fate as intimately connected to those of everyone else on the planet.

With this definition we are able to witness the capacity of a love ethic to teach us about freedom at both a personal level and a geopolitical level. When acts are taken out of fear, out of control and domination, they are not guided by a love ethic. When acts are centred from the heart and have the intention of freedom at the centre, they are guided with an ethic of interconnected love, and from this location we can sculpt more loving ways to be in this world.

bell reflects in the online interview *Speaking Freely: bell hooks* (2016) that 'living as we do in a culture of domination, to truly choose to love is heroic. To work at love, to really let yourself, you know, understand the art of loving.' She holds this reflection alongside Joseph Campbell's (2012) conception of the hero's journey and argues that we must go beyond stories of conquering and domination, and instead understand the heroic power of love.

So, as with truly loving we must love to love, not to seek an outcome. Releasing control over the outcome of what liberated futures look like, allows space for possibilities that extend beyond what our imagination, as located in the present world, can conceive of. It allows space for serendipity and deeply extends possibility. It requires us to be in a space of humility and openness to the possibilities that lie ahead. To move with the ethic of love, and to release a desire for control of the outcome of what just and liberated futures look like, calls us to move into this work from a space of deep and trusting vulnerability. Perhaps in a world that is so focused on dominating, to lead with vulnerability may be the most challenging and fear-abiding act. However, it is necessary to overcome our defences and make peace with our unknowing in order to create openings for liberatory futures that extend beyond our imaginations. So, too, to love another we must overcome fears of vulnerability and relinquish the desire to control a person, or control outcomes, so, too, to know a liberated world we must overcome these apprehensions in equal measure.

The Art of Knowing

For me, freedom requires the willingness to grow in intimacy. We must be willing to deeply know, and continue to learn and connect with, a sense of freedom and liberation to be able to enter its gates and remain within its gardens.

In *The Spirit of Intimacy*, Sobonfu Somé (2000) explores that in Dagaran communities couples must begin at the bottom of the mountain and climb up it together, this mountain being a metaphor for their relationship. It is the call to get to deeply know one another as friends, and as humans, before the stage of love is reached. This is as opposed to starting at the top of the mountain, which is what she defines as the illusion of romance because she reflects that romance 'fosters anonymity and forces people to masquerade' (p. 96). She goes on to write that 'romance means hiding our true self in order to gain acceptance' (p. 100). It is truly an art to get to deeply know another and accept them for who they are in all their complexity and contradictions, and to continually support their humanity and growth.

This is the same lens we must take to freedom. As we step deeper into freedom within ourselves, we must learn to accept the truth of who we are step by step as it unfolds. Integrating both the light and the dark. Equally, as life expands and we collectively move closer to more just futures, we must be in the work of deeply knowing and learning the intricacies of these imagined, and present, states. If we do not do the work to understand the complexity that remains on the journey to freedom, we run the risk of doing away with our progress because we want to summit the mountain immediately.

When we consider the imagination, the radical imagination, we mustn't idealise nor locate it outside of ourselves. It is both within and without. It is both perfection and imperfection.

The journey of knowing is the ability to recognise the journey is ever continuing. Just as we must continue to learn a lover as they grow, shift, and change – we too must learn to know freedom in that same way. The language we often use for this work, and the language I have also been a culprit of using throughout this book, is a language of definiteness – a language of completion. That to imagine that at some point in human history, we may achieve this state of utopic perfection, and this state we name: *freedom*.

However, as we relinquish control and live in alignment with our own authenticity and purpose, we may come to recognise that freedom is just as much here in the present as it is evasive. Our imaginations are not just a location of fictitious wonder, our imaginations are alive. Our imaginations are a dimension of reality, even if it is not concrete, yet.

So perhaps core to the work of freedom, the work of justice, is the work of presence. What is the freedom we are able to experience in the here and now, in the present moment, and how might we expand and extend that eye of freedom to the rest of our lives, and the rest of the world?

To Love

The universe is made up of matter and energy. Our political movements and strategies must equally focus on both matter and energy. The ancient sages of wisdom traditions from across the world teach us that love is the highest vibration. If we are living in loving and whole ways, we are not divorced from movement work. In the first chapter I spoke about my divestment from 'the struggle', a desire to not equate movements for change with the necessity of struggle. To give myself licence to live in the most loving and abundant way and honour my authentic expression in the world is the most radical work I can do.

To love is to heal. To heal is to love.

To emit an energy of love and of healing is to do radical and world-bending work.

It is to live in integrity with oneself, one's values, and to live a life that is reflective of those values. We must meet the energy, the vibration, of love and of freedom to meet its truest experience in our collective lives.

10

Acts of Remembering

Before we close out this journey, I want to take a moment and reorient you through time and space.

As explored, the pervading knowledge system teaches us that knowledge exists outside of us, that we must go on a journey to seek a truth, or truths, that can be grasped in the objective world. However, as I have posited, abolition and just futures are not things that exist outside of us alone, freedom is not a matter of time or of reaching to something that is beyond us.

My belief is that the reason so many of us continue to believe in a better world is because that truth is inscribed on our souls. We know deeply that something else is possible. As we witness the pain and devastation that surrounds us, the only logical response to what appears like the impossibility of justice is to fall and accept the system as it is.

Movements rely on dreaming, they rely on playing with the possible, they rely on 'illogical' solutions to the depraved problems of our world. So many of us hold a flame of hope, a flame of belief that, when we examine it, genuinely makes no sense. Makes no logical sense. Though this is the beauty of the work. Some of the greatest transformations in human history have played with the impossible, have breached the realm of what appears as illogical to the overwhelming consciousness of society. So, too, must we play with the absurd, the 'impossible'.

If we were to locate ourselves in a different time, say during the years of colonisation or slavery, to believe these ills would have come to an end would have been to believe in the impossible. Hindsight is a powerful perspective but let us not underestimate how pervasive a consciousness that witnessed these ways of being as sacrosanct was to the world. It was due to the radical dreams of our ancestors that we live in the worlds we do today.

So, too, we now live in a world where what is considered normal or necessary many of us continue to resist against and believe that something else is possible. This flame of hope, this flame of belief, I argue, is connecting with the infinite nature of our souls. There is a place each of us has found within us that believes justice is possible, when very little external to us demonstrates that.

My soul knows a better world is both possible and necessary. My soul knows that a love ethic in the world is both possible and necessary.

So, rather than considering this work as something we are striving towards, as something we are aiming to capture, I think it more apt to recognise it as something we deeply *know*. Though not something we know in a cognitive sense, something that is known through a different faculty, a different part of ourselves – a spiritual or soul-level knowing.

Abolition is an act of remembering.

Claiming more is possible in the world is an act of remembering.

Engaging deeply with our radical imagination is an act of remembering.

It is remembering that part of ourselves that the presiding knowledge system has forced us to sever in order to meet its rigid empirical validation criteria.

The art here is to go inwards, and to draw the beauty of our souls outward into the world.

Every possibility exists in the here and now, in the present moment, liberation is here – the work then, is to bring the freedom we know and experience within ourselves to the external world.

To not allow the external world to define what is possible to us. To instead recognise ourselves as the creators of this world. If we can imagine it, if we can feel into it, if we can suspend ourselves from reality as we know it and dream into different possibilities – then it is possible.

To remember that every single thing that has been created was first a seedling in the eye of someone's imagination.

So, too, can the world we are on the precipice of be a seedling germinating in your imagination today.

Let us, together, move into new possibilities of love and expand deeper into the dreams of liberation and freedom that are inscribed on our souls.

Let us remember that freedom is our birthright.

With deep and ever-enduring love,

Melz Owusu

Playlist/Outro

1. Fertile Soil – Fr33SOL, Londrelle
2. Adventure – Russ
3. Morning Asana – Londrelle
4. Blessings – Chance the Rapper (feat. Jamila Woods)
5. Manifest – Russ
6. Glory – Common, John Legend
7. Way Up – Jamila Woods
8. 444 – Gayathri Krishnan, SisterCody
9. The King's Affirmation – Iniko
10. Blessings on Blessings – OSHUN
11. sun and moon – anees
12. Solar Plexus – OSHUN
13. Vibrate Higher – Londrelle, Lalah Delia
14. Gratitude – Londrelle
15. Self-Heal – Londrelle
16. Tunnel Vision – Russ
17. i am enough – Coax Marie
18. Passion Play – Dossé-Via
19. drunk on myself – anees
20. Utah Freestyle – Russ
21. Rain Dance – Bugus, Russ

22. Grateful – Kota the Friend
23. Be Healthy – Dead Prez
24. Crystal Clear – Fr33SOL
25. Holy – Jamila Woods
26. Die Hard – Kendrick Lamar
27. Fly & Free – ByHaze, Eboni Pearce
28. Holy (Reprise) – Jamila Woods
29. The Journey – Fr33SOL
30. I Wish I Knew How It Would Feel to be Free
    – Nina Simone
31. Energy Mantra – Remix – Michael Seven
32. Angels – Chance the Rapper (feat. Saba)
33. It's Plenty – Burna Boy
34. Adventure – Russ, Rexx Life Raj
35. Demarco – I Love My Life
36. THIS YEAR (Blessings) – Victor Thompson
37. Own True Lover – melan
38. Free Spirit – Spiritual Tony
39. Khabib – Central Cee
40. Rich Spirit – Kendrick Lamar
41. Count Me Out – Kendrick Lamar
42. I Refuse – Bugus, Russ
43. Finish Line/Drown (feat. T-Pain, Kirk Franklin, Eryn
    Allen Kane, No Name)
44. Sound of Our Triumph – FR33SOL

Bibliography

Ahmed, S. (2012) *On Being Included: Racism and Diversity in Institutional Life*. Durham, NC: Duke University Press.

Alabanza, T. (2022) *None of the Above: Reflections on Life Beyond the Binary*. Edinburgh: Canongate Books.

Ames, R.T. (2017) 'Better late than never: understanding Chinese philosophy and "translating it" into the western academy', *Ethics and Education*, 12(1), 6–17.

Aurelius, M. (1800) *Meditations*. Delhi: Hachette India.

Badiou, A. (2012) *The Rebirth of History: Times of Riots and Uprisings*. London: Verso Books.

Bashford, A. and Levine, P. (2010) *The Oxford Handbook of the History of Eugenics*. New York: Oxford University Press.

BBC News (2020a) 'New college opening with degrees with no subjects', *BBC News*, 29 October. Available at: https://www.bbc.com/news/education-54725017 (accessed 25 November 2023).

BBC News (2020b) 'US 2020 Election: Does Joe Biden support defunding the police?', *BBC News*, 7 September. Available at: https://www.bbc.com/news/election-us-2020-53997196 (accessed 7 September 2022).

Berlin, I. (1969) *Two Concepts of Liberty*. Oxford: Oxford University Press.

Bhambra, G.K., Gebrial, D. and Nişancıoğlu, K. (2018) *Decolonising the University*. London: Pluto Press.

Biko, S. (1987) *I Write What I Like*. Oxford: Heinemann.

al-Bīrūnī, A.R., Kozah, M. and White, D.G. (2022) *The Yoga Sutras of Patañjali*. New York: New York University Press.

BlackPast (2012a) '(1977) The Combahee River Collective Statement', 16 November. Available at: https://www.blackpast.org/african -american-history/combahee-river-collective-statement-1977/ (accessed 25 November 2023).

BlackPast (2012b) '(1982) Audre Lorde, "Learning from the 60s"', 12 August. Available at: https://www.blackpast.org/african-a merican-history/1982-audre-lorde-learning-60s/ (accessed 25 November 2023).

Bolich, G.G. (2007) *Transgender History & Geography: Crossdressing in Context, vol. 3*. Raleigh, NC: Psyche's Press.

brown, a.m. (2017) *Emergent Strategy: Shaping Change, Changing Worlds*. Chico, CA: AK Press.

brown, a.m. (2019) *Pleasure Activism: The Politics of Feeling Good*. Chico, CA: AK Press.

brown, a.m. and Imarisha, W. (eds) (2015) *Octavia's Brood: Science Fiction Stories from Social Justice Movements*. Oakland, CA: AK Press.

Browne, K. *et al.* (2017) 'Towards transnational feminist queer methodologies', *Gender, Place and Culture: A Journal of Feminist Geography*, 24(10), 1376–97.

Burton Russell, J. (2023) *Witch hunt*. Available at: https://www.britannica.com/topic/witch-hunt (accessed 28 November 2023).

Butler, O.E. (2019a) *Parable of the Sower*. London: Headline.

Butler, O.E. (2019b) *Parable of the Talents*. London: Headline.

Cameron, J. (2016) *The Artist's Way: 30th Anniversary Edition*. New York: TarcherPerigee.

Campbell, J. (2012) *The Hero with a Thousand Faces*, 3rd edition. Novato, CA: New World Library.

Chauhan, V., Crowley, T., Fisher, A., McCabe, H. and Williams, H.

(2022) 'Losing the race? Philosophy of race in UK philosophy departments', *Metaphilosophy*, 53(1), 134–43.

Collins, P.H. (1996) 'The social construction of Black feminist thought'. In A. Garry and M. Pearsall (eds) *Women, Knowledge, and Reality*, 2nd edn. London: Routledge.

Collins, P.H. (2003) 'Toward an Afrocentric feminist epistemology'. In: Y.S. Lincoln and N.K. Denzin (eds) *Turning Points in Qualitative Research: Tying Knots in a Handkerchief*. Walnut Creek, CA: AltaMira Press, pp. 47–72.

Compton, D., Meadow, T. and Schilt, K. (2018) *Other, Please Specify: Queer Methods in Sociology*. Berkeley, CA: University of California Press.

Crenshaw, K.W. (1994) 'Mapping the margins: intersectionality, identity politics, and violence against women of color'. In M. Albertson Fineman and R. Mykitiuk (eds) *The Public Nature of Private Violence*. London: Routledge, pp. 93–118.

Currey, M. (2020) *Daily Rituals: How Great Minds Make Time, Find Inspiration, and Get to Work*. London: Picador.

Davis, A.Y. (2003) *Are Prisons Obsolete?* New York: Seven Stories Press.

de Sousa Santos, B. (2007) 'Beyond abyssal thinking: from global lines to ecologies of knowledges', *Review (Fernand Braudel Center)*, 30(1), 45–89.

de Sousa Santos, B. and Martins, B.S. (2021) *The Pluriverse of Human Rights: The Diversity of Struggles for Dignity*. New York: Routledge.

Dillon, S. (2016) '"The only freedom I can see": imprisoned queer writing and the politics of the unimaginable'. In E.A. Stanley and N. Smith (eds) *Captive Genders: Trans Embodiment and the Prison Industrial Complex*, 2nd edn. Oakland, CA: AK Press.

Dillon, S. (2018) *Fugitive Life: The Queer Politics of the Prison State*. Durham, NC: Duke University Press.

Doctor Gabor Mate: The Shocking Link Between Kindness & Illness! (2023). Available at: https://www.youtube.com/watch?v=L7zWT3 l3DV0 (accessed 29 November 2023).

Dogon Cosmology (2011). 'NASA baffled by N.W. African people!!!!!!!'.

Available at: https://www.youtube.com/watch?v=U9fJ5KnSonY (accessed 29 November 2023).

Du Plessis, P. (2021) 'Decolonisation of education in South Africa: challenges to decolonise the university curriculum', *South African Journal of Higher Education*, 35(1), 54–69.

Easwaran, E. (2007) *The Bhagavad Gita*, 2nd edn. Tomales, CA: Nilgiri Press.

Fanon, F. (2001) *The Wretched of the Earth*, translated by C. Farrington. New York: Penguin Classics.

Fanon, F. (2008) *Black Skin, White Masks*, revised edn. London: Pluto Press.

Federici, S. (2021) *Caliban and the Witch: Women, the Body and Primitive Accumulation*. London: Penguin Books.

Foucault, M. (2020) *Discipline and Punish: The Birth of the Prison*. London: Penguin.

Freire, P. (2017) *Pedagogy of the Oppressed*. London: Penguin.

Fukuyama, F. (2020) *The End of History and the Last Man*. Harmondsworth: Penguin.

Garland, D. (2014) 'What is a "history of the present"? On Foucault's genealogies and their critical preconditions', *Punishment & Society*, 16(4), 365–84.

Gilmore, R.W. (2007) *Golden Gulag Prisons, Surplus, Crisis, and Opposition in Globalizing California*. Berkeley, CA: University of California Press.

Go, J. (2013) 'Part II: Decolonizing sociology'. In J. Go (ed.) *Decentering Social Theory*. Bingley: Emerald Publishing.

Go, J. (2017) 'Decolonizing sociology: epistemic inequality and socio-logical thought', *Social Problems*, 64(2), 194–9.

Gottcke, L.M. (2020) 'The end and continuation of history: Zadie Smith's critique of Francis Fukuyama in *White Teeth*', *Critique: Studies in Contemporary Fiction*, 61(2), 219–35.

Grosfoguel, R. (2013) 'The structure of knowledge in Westernized universities: epistemic racism/sexism and the four genocides/epistemicides of the long 16th century', *Human Architecture*, 11(1), 73–90.

Guzmán Valenzuela, C. (2021) 'Disrupting curricula and pedagogies in Latin American universities: six criteria for decolonising the university', *Teaching in Higher Education*, 26(7–8), 1019–37.

Halberstam, J. (2018) *Female Masculinity*. Durham, NC: Duke University Press.

Harney, S. and Moten, F. (2013) *The Undercommons: Fugitive Planning & Black Study*. New York: Minor Compositions.

Hartman, S. (2019) *Wayward Lives, Beautiful Experiments: Intimate Histories of Social Upheaval*. New York: W.W. Norton.

Hirst, P. (1989) 'Endism', *The London Review of Books*, 11(22), 14.

HISTORY (2023) 'African Tribe's SHOCKING Origin Story in the Stars | Ancient Aliens (Season 1)'. Available at: https://www.youtube.com/watch?v=GX5bZvuD6kE (accessed 25 November 2023).

Hobbes, T. (1929 [1651]) *Hobbes's Leviathan*, reprint edn. Oxford: Oxford University Press.

Hoff, B.H. (2014) 'Unseen art scene: issues of homosexuality', *Unseen Art Scene*, 2 August. Available at: https://africanartists.blogspot.com/2014/08/issues-of-homosexuality.html (accessed 29 November 2023).

hooks, b. (1994) *Teaching to Transgress: Education as the Practice of Freedom*. New York: Routledge.

hooks, b. (2018) *All About Love: New Visions*. New York: William Morrow.

Imarisha, W. (2013) 'Minefields; after the revolution', *Capitalism, Nature, Socialism*, 24(4), 123–5.

Jahi, J. (2014) 'Why isn't my professor black? | UCL Events'. Available at: https://blogs.ucl.ac.uk/events/2014/03/21/whyisntmyprofessorblack/ (accessed 25 November 2023).

James, J. (2013) 'Afrarealism and the Black matrix: Maroon philosophy at democracy's border', *The Black Scholar*, 43(4), 124–31.

Jung, C.G. (1978) *Man and His Symbols*. London: Pan Books.

Jung, C.G. (1981) *The Archetypes and The Collective Unconscious*, 2nd edition, translated by R.F.C. Hull. Princeton, NJ: Princeton University Press.

Kaba, M. (2021) *We Do This 'Til We Free Us: Abolitionist Organizing and Transforming Justice*. Edited by T.K. Nopper. Chicago, IL: Haymarket Books.

Kant, I. (2011) *Observations on the Feeling of the Beautiful and Sublime and Other Writings*. Edited and translated by P. Frierson and P. Guyer. Cambridge: Cambridge University Press (Cambridge Texts in the History of Philosophy).

Kelley, R.D.G. (2022) *Freedom Dreams: The Black Radical Imagination*. Boston, MA: Beacon Press.

Kwoba, B., Chantiluke, R. and Nkopo, A. (2018) *Rhodes Must Fall: The Struggle to Decolonise the Racist Heart of Empire*. London: Bloomsbury Academic.

Levin, S. (2020) 'The movement to defund police has won historic victories across the US. What's next?', *The Guardian*, 15 August. Available at: https://www.theguardian.com/us-news/2020/aug/15/defund-police-movement-us-victories-what-next (accessed 7 September 2022).

Lorde, A. (2013) 'Uses of the erotic'. In: *Sister Outsider: Essays and Speeches*, reprint edn. Berkeley, CA: Ten Speed Press, pp. 53–9.

Maldonado-Torres, N. (2004) 'The topology of being and the geo-politics of knowledge: modernity, empire, coloniality', *City*, 8(1), 29–56.

Meghji, A. (2021) *Decolonizing Sociology: An Introduction*. Cambridge: Polity.

Middleton, J. (2004) 'Spirit possession among the Lugbara'. In J. Beattie and J. Middleton (eds) *Spirit Mediumship and Society in Africa*. London: Routledge, pp. 258–69.

Mill, J.S. (2016) *On Liberty*. CreateSpace Independent Publishing Platform.

Mills, C.W. (2022) *The Racial Contract*, 2nd edn. Ithaca, NY: Cornell University Press.

Milne, S. (2012) *The Revenge of History: The Battle for the 21st Century*. London: Verso.

Munoz, J.E. (2009) *Cruising Utopia: The Then and There of Queer Futurity*. New York: NYU Press.

Nash, C.J. and Browne, K. (2010) *Queer Methods and Methodologies: Intersecting Queer Theories and Social Science Research*. London: Taylor & Francis.

Outlaw Jr., L.T. and Jeffers, C. (2022) 'Africana philosophy', in E.N. Zalta and U. Nodelman (eds) *The Stanford Encyclopedia of Philosophy*. Fall 2022. Metaphysics Research Lab, Stanford University. Available at: https://plato.stanford.edu/archives/fall2 022/entries/africana/ (accessed 25 November 2023).

Owusu, M. (2020) 'One year on testosterone: time, spirituality, and the (un)gendering of Blackness', *Medium*, 29 April. Available at: https://medium.com/@melzowusu/one-year-on-testosterone-time-spirituality-and-the-un-gendering-of-blackness-d2af8b23 1ad2 (accessed 25 November 2023).

Peck, M.S. (2003) *The Road Less Traveled: A New Psychology of Love, Traditional Values and Spiritual Growth*. Anniversary edition. New York: Touchstone.

Pemberton, A. and Kisamore, J. (2023) 'Assessing burnout in diversity and inclusion professionals', *Equality, Diversity and Inclusion: An International Journal*, 42(1), 38–52.

Rancière, J. (1974) 'On the theory of ideology: The politics of Althusser', *Radical Philosophy*, 007. Available at: https://www.radicalphilosophy.com/article/on-the-theory-of-ideology (accessed 25 November 2023).

Reiter, B. (2018) *Constructing the Pluriverse: The Geopolitics of Knowledge*. Durham, NC: Duke University Press.

Rick Rubin: The 60 Minutes Interview (2023). Available at: https://www.youtube.com/watch?v=EUbUn9FnrME (accessed 20 November 2023).

Rubin, R. (2023) *The Creative Act: A Way of Being*. New York: Penguin Books.

Said, E.W. (2003) *Orientalism*. London: Penguin Books.

Science Channel (2023) *Did the Dogon Tribe Predict What Stars Are Made Of?! | NASA's Unexplained Files*. Available at: https://www.youtube.com/watch?v=NuDKw7jpyOc (accessed 25 November 2023).

Sharpe, C. (2016) *In the Wake: On Blackness and Being*. Durham, NC: Duke University Press.

Shilliam, R. (2021) *Decolonizing Politics: An Introduction*. Cambridge: Polity.

Snorton, C.R. (2017) *Black on Both Sides: A Racial History of Trans Identity*. Minneapolis, MN: University of Minnesota Press.

Somé, M.P. (1995) *Of Water and the Spirit: Ritual, Magic, and Initiation in the Life of an African Shaman*, reprint edn. New York: TarcherPerigee.

Somé, S. (2000) *The Spirit of Intimacy: Ancient Teachings in the Ways of Relationships*. New York: William Morrow & Company.

Speaking Freely: bell hooks (2016). Available at: https://www.youtube.com/watch?v=g2bmnwehlpA (accessed 25 November 2023).

Spivak, G.C. (2004) 'Can the subaltern speak?' In *Imperialism*. London: Routledge.

Waite, S. (2015) 'Cultivating the scavenger: a queerer feminist future for composition and rhetoric'. Available at: https://cfshrc.org/article/cultivating-the-scavenger-a-queerer-feminist-future-for-composition-and-rhetoric/ (accessed 11 August 2021).

Woods, A. (2022) 'Why many DEI leaders are experiencing burnout and how you can fix it', *Inc.com*. Available at: https://www.inc.com/arthur-woods/why-many-dei-leaders-are-experiencing-burnout-how-you-can-fix-it.html (accessed 21 October 2022).

Wortham, J. (2020) 'How a new wave of Black activists changed the conversation', *The New York Times*, 25 August. Available at: https://www.nytimes.com/2020/08/25/magazine/black-visions-collective.html (accessed 7 September 2022).

Zaru, D. and Simpson, T. (2020) '"Defund the police" movement 6 months after killing of George Floyd', *ABC News*. Available at: https://abcnews.go.com/US/defund-police-movement-months-killing-george-floyd/story?id=74296015 (accessed 7 September 2022).

Zhang, C. (2013) 'Critique against "End of History"', *Wuhan li gong da xue xue bao. She hui ke xue ban*, 26(1), 97–100. Available at: https://doi.org/10.3963/j.issn.1671-6477.2013.01.019.

Index